Journey to Jesus

Volume One: Quest for Life

Journey to Jesus

Volume One: Quest for Life

James Stone

WINEPRESS WP PUBLISHING

Unless otherwise noted all scriptures are taken from the King James Version of the Bible.

Verses marked NIV are taken from the Holy Bible, New International Version, Copyright © 1973, 1978, 1984 by the International Bible Society. Used by permission of Zondervan Publishing House. The "NIV" and "New International Version" trademarks are registered in the United States Patent and Trademark Office by International Bible Society.

Verses marked NKJV are taken from the New King James Version, Copyright © 1979, 1980, 1982 by Thomas Nelson, Inc., Publishers. Used by permission.

ISBN 1-57921-284-0
Library of Congress Catalog Card Number: 00-100108

journey to jesus—the series

The series, *Journey to Jesus,* is the continuing story of the revelation of the grace of God, the sovereign power of God at work in the world. Beginning with elementary explanations of the manifestation and the frustration of the grace of God, it concludes with the books *Being Set Free* and *Reaching the Heart.* It is the saga of one man's struggle (which, perhaps, mirrors the struggles of all men) to come to terms with Jesus Christ as the sole way of life.

Provocative and challenging to the belief system of much of modern Christianity, the revelation of God's grace moves man to rekindle his focus upon Jesus Christ. It brings man to view his Creator, not as the object of man's obsessions, but rather as the inherent fiber of his existence. The idolatry of man's self-centeredness, even when God is the end of all of man's actions, is brought into question by the revelation of the grace of God. The freedom which man has been inherently given is understood in the light of the sovereignty of God's grace.

Journey to Jesus captures the continual struggle of man to believe that Jesus Christ is the sole essence of life. It is the story of man being saved from himself, the proclamation that Jesus, and Jesus alone, is life!

a c k n o w l e d g m e n t s

I appreciate all the help I received in preparing the manuscript, especially the investment of time by those who read rough drafts; and Janis King, in particular. Ultimately, the groundwork of any experience that occurs in my life lies in the love of my family: my wife of thirty-six years, Louise; my children, Dana and her husband, Marion; Shawn and his wife, Robinn, with their daughter, Brittany; and Keisha and her husband, Roger Hunt, with their daughters, Raven and Amber, and son, Joshua. My prayer is that grace might be multiplied unto them for, unfortunately, my resistance to God is always acted out within the framework of their lives.

contents

preface

The breath of life is like a golden thread that weaves its way through every fiber of man's life. Often undetected by the consciousness of man's mind, it nevertheless constantly influences, and ultimately controls, the living of man's life. It is the heartbeat of every action, for man continually strives for the ultimate manifestation of life that can be experienced.

Sadly, however, since there is mystery in life, all men eventually struggle with simply living. Although every man is driven from within to experience the rich, full, and complete life, it becomes, for most, an elusive dream. The proverbial carrot, which is continually dangled in front of man's hungering eyes, is never caught. When life comes to the end of its days for most people, too many songs have not been sung, too many books have not been written, and too many noble deeds have not been done. Very few people ever experience the power of the true intimacy of life. The glory of what should have been is never experienced.

Every man has been graced to experience the ultimate expression of life. When a newborn inhales its first breath of air, the miracle of life begins. But life is more than the breathing of air by the body, which is miracle enough for the wonder of man. Something far more grand has occurred. A robe of flesh has been incarnated with the Spirit of God. Man has been graced to experience the life of God.

Experiencing that life is not only man's greatest moment, it is also his greatest challenge. The free flow of the grace of God is the issue of life. For man, it is, in reality, the quest to know Jesus—the quest for life. Since grace is the provision that God gives to His creation to enable them to experience life, grace in its ultimate definition is Jesus. Jesus is the provision by which all men live.

One of the major areas of concern, if not the top priority, in modern Christianity is the need to return to Jesus as the breath and heartbeat of life itself. With the market flooded with how-to books and formulas to gain the heart of God, Jesus, the only way to the Father, has been relegated to a secondary role at best.

Stirring, charismatic preachers give their newfound formula for success. Then, almost as an afterthought, they say that only Jesus "anoints" or makes the formula work. The difference between Jesus helping or anointing the believer to live, and Jesus being the actual breath and heartbeat of the believer's life, is the issue that has plagued mankind since the Garden of Eden. It is the difference between religion (religion being defined as what man does for or to God) and the true way of God, Jesus Christ.

Although all men have been graced to experience the life of God, most men fail to experience that life because grace is bestowed upon them in vain (1 Cor. 15:10; 2 Cor. 6:1). Surprisingly, the pursuit of life by man always frustrates the grace of God in man. Paul seemed to express that thought when he wrote to the Romans concerning the Jews: "For they being ignorant of God's righteousness, and going about to establish their own righteousness, have not submitted themselves unto the righteousness of God" (Rom. 10:3). Is it not the "going about to establish their own righteousness" that prohibited them from "submitting themselves unto the righteousness of God"? Mysteriously, man's pursuit of life always frustrates the life of God already given to him.

The only cure for the "messenger of Satan" (2 Cor. 12:7; also compare Matt. 16:23), which keeps inflicting its deadly wound upon the heart of man, is the revelation of the grace of God. It is only the gospel of Jesus Christ (the good news proclaiming that God the Father has sent His Son into the believer's life to baptize him with His Spirit, in order to take the believer where he could not go himself) that saves and keeps man (1 Cor. 15:1–2). The only way man will ever be changed, and stay changed, is having the free flow of the grace of God that dwells within him. Jesus Christ is the only Way to complete successfully, the quest for life.

i n t r o d u c t i o n

Like the water that plunges over the falls, the river of life—the flowing of the grace of God—carries every man to his destiny. The experiencing of life which occurs either in the manifestation of grace or the frustration of grace, dictates to man his actions and reactions. For man is driven from deep within the essence of his being to seek continually the fullest possible expression of life. Whether he understands it or not, every man is on a journey—the journey to Jesus, who is the ultimate expression of life for mankind.

Although this journey of life begins with such hope and glory, it soon turns, quicker for some than others, to despair and shame. Most, if not all, men eventually struggle with life because there is mystery in experiencing the rich, full, complete life. Surprisingly, man's pursuit of life destroys the life of God already given to him.

The apostle Paul summarized this profound truth when he wrote to first-century believers in the church in Rome. He said, ". . . the wages of sin is death; but the gift of God is eternal life through Jesus Christ our Lord" (Rom. 6:23). Man earns his "hells," the wages of lost innocence; however, he does not merit his "heavens." The rich, full, abundant life is not the product of the pursuit of man. It is the unmerited gift of God. As Jesus said, "Ye have not chosen me, but I have chosen you . . ." (John 15:16). Mysteriously, the fulfillment of life for man comes not from the pursuit of life by man; rather, it comes from the pursuit of man by life.

Such is the story of my life. After forty years of religious pursuits, I now see the error of my ways. I can express it only by saying that some way Jesus broke through to me and arrested me. I am now continually being saved because God is continually conquering me.

As a result of this rescue of my life, I now see Jesus more distinctly as ". . . the way, the truth, and the life" (John 14:6). This redemptive revelation has delivered me from the bondage of seeing Jesus as the object of my devotion, my piety, and my worship. I now know that if there is any true (spiritual, as opposed to fleshly) devotion, piety, or worship in my life, it is there because Jesus is the devotion, Jesus is the piety, and Jesus is the worship. Jesus Christ is the life and light of all men (John 1:4, 9).

This true revelation of Jesus Christ can be illustrated in another way. I can say, "My faith is in Jesus." Do I mean, *"My* faith is in Jesus?" Or do I mean, "My faith is *in* Jesus?"

My faith always produces my devotion, my piety, and my worship. My faith only produces my attempt to be more zealous, more holy, and more serving to and for God. Whereas, being in Jesus, He is always faithful to do what He said He would do. The faithfulness of God is as sure as the essence of God Himself.

I am justified (rendered innocent, as "freedom from guile or cunning: simplicity"—the literal meaning of the original word is translated *innocence* in the New Testament by the KJV) by the faithfulness of God. The true faith now manifested in my life is the miracle (the faithless now experiencing faith) and mystery (the breathless now experiencing breath) of life. His faithfulness, His glory, and His life are being reflected in me.

With the understanding that Jesus Christ is my life and light (John 1:1–14; Acts 17:22–29; Isa. 42:5; Prov. 20:27; and John 14:6), the quest to know Him, then, has become the challenge of life itself. Because every man has an innate desire to experience the rich, full, and complete life, the quest to know Jesus is the challenge of every man's life. Although this inner craving of man is largely misunderstood and seldom fully realized, it is, nevertheless, the driving force that propels man to seek the fullest possible expression of life. Mysteriously, all men seek Jesus. They seek life, the life of God.

Within this mystery of what it means to be a living soul, man finds himself struggling continually for his physical and/or emotional survival. Whether it is understood or not, every man is on a journey, a spiritual journey, to experience the quickening power of life itself. Jesus said:

It is like a grain of mustard seed, which, when it is sown in the earth, is less than all the seeds that be in the earth: But when it is sown, it groweth up, and becometh greater than all herbs, and shooteth out great branches; so that the fowls of the air may lodge under the shadows of it (Mark 4:31–32).

Knowing Jesus Christ is a journey that moves the seeker or learner of life from an understanding that is "less than all the seeds that be in the earth" to become "greater than all herbs, and shooteth out great branches." The quest to know Jesus is the quest to know the rich, full, completed life.

Life in this journey to Jesus can be illustrated by the germinating relationship between a man and a woman. When the relationship begins, it, too, is like the smallest of seeds planted in one's life. Yet if the relationship is allowed to grow to maturity, the process, the growing together of two to become one, becomes the greatest event of their lives.

It becomes an exciting challenge to live life in the learning of each other. For when both members of the relationship continually experience the growing process, the knowing of each other then becomes a never-ending noble adventure in the experiencing of life. The joy of life is always in the knowing of another.

Moreover, the relationship formed between the man and the woman actually becomes greater than the sum of the two individuals. It radiates life, not just to the two, but to all those who "may lodge under the shadows of it." This process of moving from the smallest of seeds to the greatest of herbs, the quest to know each other, as the quest to know Jesus Christ, becomes the greatest event of life.

The successful achieving of this journey to life is uniquely Christian. It is intricately involved in the experiencing of Jesus Christ. In other words, the emphasis of life is actually upon the learning process rather than what is being learned. This is not to say that what is being learned or being experienced is not important. Rather, it implies that how one learns is more important.

Mysteriously, the process of the learning experience itself is the essence of life. For when one stops learning, he begins to die—even though he now has a vast resource of things that have been learned. Incredibly, tragically, it has always been the people of God, the people who have once experienced God and learned about Him who eventually experience death.

In other words, the relationship between most believers and Christ, as with most relationships between men and women, stagnate and cease to be an exciting adventure. They become stale and lifeless. Sadly, the relationship becomes a deadly boredom that subjects the individuals to the temptation to find life somewhere else.

For the Christian, as with the man and the woman, to experience continual (perpetual, eternal) life, life must not be attempted by living in past experiences, as glorious as they may be. Abundant life is not based upon what has happened, but rather upon what is now being experienced. Continual, abundant life can be found only in the current learning of Christ, only in being a disciple of Jesus Christ.

A learner (disciple) of Jesus Christ is not one who has learned something (such as a glorious truth or even a glorious experience) and then attempts to live life based upon that knowledge or event. Rather, it is to base life upon the learning process itself. Simply stated, a disciple of Christ is a learner, as opposed to being one who has learned. Eternal (perpetual) life is to experience the eternal (perpetual) learning of Jesus.

Jesus spoke of this mystery of the continual learning process when He said:

> *Is a candle brought to be put under a bushel, or under a bed? and not to be set on a candlestick? For there is nothing hid, which shall not be manifested; neither was any thing kept secret, but that it should come abroad. If any man have ears to hear, let him hear. And he said unto them, Take heed what ye hear; with what measure ye mete, it shall be measured to you; and unto you that hear shall more be given. For he that hath, to him shall be given: and he that hath not, from him shall be taken even that which he hath* (Mark 4:21–25).

Failure to experience the perpetual, contented life is not a problem of the amount of knowledge obtained, but rather a problem of failing to experience the learning process itself continually.

With the coming of the God-Man, Jesus Christ, all that is necessary to experience the continual, perpetual life has been manifested. Nothing has been held back by the Father in the giving of His Son. Obviously, however, since His coming, many have not experienced that abundant life. Moreover, many have experienced the vibrant, victorious life of Christ but have lost their vitality. ("He that hath not, from him shall be taken even that which he hath.") Although still a Christian in the sense of being an adopted son of God, they no longer experience the wealth of the life that should be in Christ.

The continual experiencing of the learning process, continually having an ear to hear, produces the continual experience of the abundant life. ("For he that hath, to him shall be given.") On the other hand, if the hearing ear becomes deaf, the believer not only stops hearing, but he loses the vibrant, victorious life he was experiencing. Failing to hear continually, he dies.

As Paul implied, man has been created as such that "[he has] this treasure [life in Christ] in earthen vessels, that the excellency of the power [the capability to produce life] may be of God, and not of [man]" (2 Cor. 4:7). The power to produce life never becomes an attribute of the vessel. It always remains with the Source of life, the treasure within the vessel. It is only the continual hearing of the treasure that enables the vessel to experience the continual life of Christ.

Unfortunately, since the inception of evil into that which was good (the fall of Lucifer, the celestial cherub), creation has attempted to live life in what has been learned or experienced. In other words, the vessel experiencing the attributes of life from the treasure attempts to live life in those attributes themselves, forsaking the One who has produced the attributes.

Experiencing the forbidden fruit of "the tree of the knowledge of good and evil" (Gen. 2:17), man has become trapped in the knowledge of having experienced abundant life but is now unable to reproduce it. At best, he has learned to cope with his plight to produce a somewhat stable society and to prevent total insanity. At worst, he has become a raving lunatic.

Thus, salvation for man is the journey back from the various regions of insanity, to complete mental control by the Spirit. It is a journey back to life in the treasure, Jesus Christ, as opposed to the attempt to find life in what has been produced by Jesus. It is a journey back to life in the Spirit.

Moreover, the journey back is a continual struggle, because man, once experiencing the fruit "of the tree of the knowledge of good and evil," simply does not want to give up his perception that he is a "god" (Gen. 3:22). He has become self-centered (taking one's own creatureliness to be the center, object, and norm of all experience) rather than Creator-centered: "Wherefore God also gave them up to uncleanness through the lusts of their own hearts, to dishonour their own bodies between themselves: Who changed the truth of God into a lie, and worshipped and served the creature more than the Creator, who is blessed for ever. Amen" (Rom. 1:24–25).

This book endeavors to tell the story of my journey back to Jesus Christ. It is a story of my movement back to a godly way of life. It is a record of my need to die continually to my self-centeredness and truly become God-centered.

As I draw closer to my sixtieth year, one thing has become increasingly clear. In the deep regions of my inner self, I find one who does not want to give up his throne, his self-centeredness. Although the experiences of life keep forcing me to change my outward behavior in order to have a more stable existence with the least amount of trouble from others, I always seem to scheme myself back into being the "god" of my life. I find my self-centeredness rising again and again.

Now I can grasp, perhaps, what Jeremiah meant when he said, "The heart is deceitful above all things and desperately wicked: who can know it?" (Jer. 17:9). Now I understand with a much clearer revelation, God's statement after the great flood, "I will never again curse the ground for man's sake, even though every inclination of his heart is evil from childhood . . ." (Gen. 8:21). By God's mercy and grace, I now confess that the heart of James "is deceitful above all things" and "every inclination of [my] heart is evil from childhood."

Even now with God's mercy and grace, it is painful for me to confess those words. Moreover, I know that this confession is so agonizing and destructive to my self-centeredness that I will, at the first chance, devise schemes that allow me to deny my wickedness. I keep striving to understand and to develop a doctrine that will allow me to feel good about myself from within myself, instead of having a sense of well being from being in Christ.

I will even create a teaching that will give God credit for making me feel good about myself. I simply will not give up my throne. Perhaps this is what David meant when he said, "[The wicked] plot injustice and say, 'We have devised a perfect plan!' Surely the mind and heart of man are cunning" (Ps. 64:6 NIV). Unless God continually works in my life, I will forever rule my throne and scheme cleverly devised plans to keep me there.

Paradoxically, I will proclaim that I live righteously, I have understanding, I seek God, and I am a good person. Even though Scripture states, "As it is written: 'There is none righteous, no, not one; There is none who understands; there is none who seeks after God. They have all turned aside; they have together become unprofitable; there is none who does good, no, not one'" (Rom. 3:10–12 NKJV). Most assuredly, those characteristics do not refer to me, for I have chosen to give my life to God. Or do they?

Alas, could it also be true that ". . . my throat is an open tomb and my tongue practices deceit"? Is "my mouth full of cursing and bitterness"? Are "my feet swift to shed blood"? Has "destruction and misery been in my way"? Is "the way of peace not known by me"? Is "there really no fear of God before my eyes"? Am I really "guilty before God"? (Rom. 3:13–19, paraphrased). Sadly, in those rare moments of honesty, I have to confess, yes, that is me!

Although I have learned to modify my behavior to mask my real self-centeredness, I am basically driven by my selfish vanity. To keep from being too abrasive, and thus totally alienating everyone around me, I have learned to play the role of caring for others. I now see that I have continually used others to meet my narcissism, however. Begrudgingly, I have to admit I have been driven by the continual need of having my self-centeredness stroked, my inner self lifted up.

Hear me out. Do not shut me off yet. I have worked for God. I have spent many hours building His church. I have traveled across America and several other countries, proclaiming the message of God. I have been Spirit-filled as on the day of Pentecost, experienced and witnessed divine healing, participated in the exorcism of unclean spirits. I have helped those in need. My family and I have sacrificed for God.

Moreover, I have faithfully done as the church has said. I have been baptized in water, participated in communion, washed the saints' feet, and practiced all the other essentials of the church. I have assembled together with other believers, paid my tithes, and spent many hours in fasting and praying.

Finally, I have kept the law. I have practiced the rulings of my tradition. I have faithfully lived by the teaching of the church and adhered to the advice given. I obeyed "those over me in the Lord" (Heb. 13:17). Abraham may not have been justified by his works, rituals, or law (Rom. 4), but surely my efforts will not go unrewarded, for I have given my life to God and His church.

Perplexed, I wonder, in view of all my labors, why do I have no lasting peace? Why am I not undisturbed by the storms of life? Why do I seem to be like a yo-yo that rises and falls by the forces of nature that work upon me? Why am I constantly driven by every wind of adversity that comes against me?

I rejoice in my zeal to work for God. The challenge of doing or becoming what I want to be excites my inner drives. The joy of beginning a new task, a new plan for accomplishments, a new initiation of effort to find glory, floods my soul.

Yet, seemingly, I never reach the goal. I wilt under the hot sun of affliction. There is little, if any, hope that I can ever make it to the top. I lose my sense of direction.

Although discouragement sometimes overwhelms me, I will not succumb to its deception. I will ascend beyond its deadly depths. I will rise above its tentacles. I will climb over its obstacles. I will rise again to give the best of my effort, to give the best of myself for the cause of Christ. I will be victorious!

Yet, in the midst of my dreams and aspirations, I have this submerged apprehension that forces itself into my awareness every so often: I am without strength, I am ungodly, I am a sinner. Sometimes I feel I am really on the opposite side of God. I have an overwhelming sense of guilt that I have not arrived. I am dying from within my soul.

The only sense of relief I have is to experience the forgiveness of God's love. The cycle becomes tedious, however. Even the cry, "It's me again, Lord. I have failed," grows wearisome. I find myself tiring of the endless succession of failures and absolutions. Is there no ultimate victory?

I learned that ultimate victory would come in my "death." I learned I must die to sin. I must die to self. I must live the crucified life. I must reckon myself to be dead to sin but alive to God. I must not yield my members as instruments of unrighteousness to sin. I must yield myself to God. I must identify with the death and resurrection of Jesus Christ.

Yet, in all my attempting to be "dead," I still find myself living. All I have to do is to take an honest look at myself, not at the image of what I am trying to believe in my mind, but the reality of what is happening in my inner self. I do not find the fruits of holiness (life) but the wages of sin (death). My peace, joy, and rest are often pushed aside for gloom, despair, and agony. In the still moments of the night, after the busy activities of my frantic efforts subside, the real essence of my being reveals that something is wrong. In those still moments, the wages of sin (stress, despair, a sense of being forsaken and destroyed) bear heavily upon me.

I, as it seemed with Paul, often find myself in a dilemma: "For that which I do I allow not: for what I would, that do I not; but what I hate, that do I" (Rom. 7:15). Certainly, ". . . to will is present with me; but how to perform that which is good I find not" (Rom. 7:18). Oh, ". . . I delight in the law of God after the inward man: but I see another law in my members, warring against the law of my mind, and bringing me into captivity to the law of sin which is in my members" (Rom. 7:22–23). "O wretched man that I am! who shall deliver me from the body of this death?" (Rom. 7:24).

Who shall deliver me? What a question! Suddenly a ray of light pierced my soul. "Who shall deliver me" has never been my question.

I have always asked, "How can I get out of the mess I have made?" "Who will help me fix the problems of my life?" "How can I solve the struggles of my existence?" I have even tried to use God as a means of my solution.

As this burst of light penetrated the wall of darkness within me, amazing truth drove itself into the intercessions of my heart. Understanding mysteriously began to break forth upon my reasoning. My eyes began to see rays of enlightenment. I slowly grasped the deeper things of life.

The difference between my questions and the question, "Who shall deliver me," broke forth into my inner being as the secret of life. It is the difference between deadly religiosity and true believers in Christ. One is a cry of the individual for deliverance from the circumstances. The other is a cry to be saved from himself. One is an attempt to use God as a personal source for one's accomplishments. The other is the realization of one's total incompetence. One is the working of a "schemer" keeping himself involved in the things of God. The other is understanding who is the problem. One is death. The other is life. The struggle of the two brings forth the beginning exploration into the mysteries of grace.

What a dilemma of futility to know the real self-centeredness of one's self. In perhaps the most thorough and precise statement on the issue of life ever written by man, the Epistle to the Romans, Paul clearly stated the plight of man to ever come to know himself. He simply wrote, "for we know not . . ." (8:26).

He did not make this statement in Romans 3, where he stated, "For all have sinned, and come short of the glory of God" (v. 23). It stands to reason that this chapter, where it is revealed that all men have sinned, should be the place where Paul would write: "for we know not." Yet he did not state it here.

Neither did he make the statement in Romans 4, where he proclaimed that Abraham was not justified by works, rituals, or the law. If one attempts to approach God in the wrong manner, he certainly could be identified as not knowing. The statement is not found here, however.

Likewise, he did not make the statement in Romans 5, the justification chapter. Nor is the statement made in Romans 6, the sanctification chapter, with its emphasis on knowing that one is set apart for God. It seems that both chapters could be the place where he stated, "for we know not." Yet it is not found in either of those chapters.

Paul did not even make the statement in Romans 7, the "I cannot do as I ought to" chapter. One might assume that this would be the place where Paul stated, "for we know not." Again it is not.

Amazingly, Paul actually said, "for we know not" in Romans 8, the Spirit-filled chapter, where Paul eulogizes life in the Spirit. Surely the Spirit-filled Christian should know his own heart, but Paul said, "Likewise the Spirit also helpeth our infirmities: for we know not what we should pray for as we ought: but the Spirit itself maketh intercession for us with groanings which cannot be uttered" (8:26).

Notice the painful similarity between Paul's statement, "for we know not . . .," and Jeremiah's statement, "The heart of man is deceitful above all things and desperately wicked: who can know it?" (Jer. 17:9). After forty years of being a Christian, surely I should know for what I should pray. I find that when I pray as I think I should pray, however, it is always to feed the love of my self-centeredness. Vainly I pray for my own enhancement. Painfully, I have come to realize I, too, "know not what [I] should pray for as [I] ought."

Could the statements of Jeremiah (before Christ) and of Paul (after Christ) actually mean that the heart of man will never change? My self-centeredness trembles at the thought. I adamantly proclaim my heart has been changed! I have been made a "new creature." I have been a Christian for over forty years!

But has it? Oh, in high moments of religiosity, I boldly proclaim, "I have been changed." In the reality of day-to-day living, however, wickedness keeps raising its ugly head. All the struggles of my life that I previously enumerated are a testament that my heart has not been changed.

I must confess that I can never know my heart, my true "inner self," other than it is wicked. Like men of old, I desperately, continually devise plans to keep me on my throne. At worst, I completely ignore my Creator and live as I dictate. At best, I mix grace and law in order to attempt to meet the demands of the Creator, but also yield to the demands of my self-centeredness. I desperately desire the workings of God but, unfortunately, only to enhance my own being. It seems my heart ". . . plot[s] injustice and say[s], '[I] have devised a perfect plan!' [My] mind and heart . . . are cunning" (Ps. 64:6 NIV).

After over forty years of being a Christian, how painful it is to say that my heart is still wicked. Although I have tried religiously to change my heart, it has not changed. I, too, cannot do as I would.

There is hope, however. The good news of Jesus Christ proclaims that the hope for every believer is not the changing of a heart. It is not the remaking of an old heart. The old heart will never change. It will always be desperately wicked and cunning in its scheming. It just learns to be religious, to "play the game," as if it has been changed.

The good news is that in Christ there is the creation of a new heart for man. The believer now lives as if he has a new heart, because he now experiences life in the heart of Christ. He has a new heart, not because his heart is made over or made new. His old heart is continually dying, yet he experiences the life of a new heart because he now lives in the heart of Christ.

The only answer for my deceitful heart is a new heart. I must experience a "heart transplant" from life in my heart, to life in the heart of Christ. I must experience the exchanged life, Christ's heart for my heart. Although my heart remains in me, it no longer serves as the essence of my life. It must continually die off. Christ now becomes the essence of my life. He must continually live.

In experiencing this exchanging of the hearts, one of the most profound mysteries of grace has been revealed. Just as I fought my conversion experience of being moved out of myself and back into Jesus, my heart continually, desperately schemes to put me back on the throne of my life. Even after conversion, my heart resists the sovereign power of God.

It is a resistance that always fails, however. Moreover, the failure is always twofold. First, my resistance to the sovereign power of God fails to produce the life that I thought it would. Second, my resistance always ends when I begin to experience the only consequence for that resistance, my spiritual death. Unless I have become a reprobate (by continually "blasphem[ing] against the Holy Ghost" [Mark 3:29; Rev. 9:20, 16:9, 11]), my resistance to the sovereign power of God always begins to subside, amazingly, yet not so amazingly, when I near the tragic "end of myself." Turning from God always produces the pressure that brings me back to God.

God's love for me is so complete, so perfect that He always lets me turn from Him. Oh, He weeps for me in my rejection (Luke 19:41), but, nevertheless, He allows me to reject His love. For without the freedom of rejection, His love would be nothing more than the selfish gratification of a personal desire. True love always gives the freedom to be rejected.

Who would reject the love of God? Certainly it would never be by choice. I know my rejection of His love was never by choice. When the alternatives of life (love) and death (apathy) are before me, I never purposely choose "not to live." No man purposely chooses the death of his true life. Even suicide is a testament to the value of life by attempting to end a life that is not experiencing life.

Deception is the only thing that causes me to turn from life to death. I will be deceived into thinking that something other than Jesus Christ, the Way, can produce my life. Although the enemy can use many things in the deception, those things only tempt me because I want the perceived choice of what is good and what is evil for my life. Ultimately, I am continually deceived in thinking that I can produce life.

Now, I know that in spite of myself, by the grace of God, I will be brought back into Jesus. Jesus said, "And I, if I be lifted up from the earth, will draw all men unto me" (John 12:32). With the literal meaning of the word translated *draw* being "to drag," it reveals the true story of my life, the true story of the way of Christ. The sovereign power of God is literally dragging me back into Jesus Christ.

If Jesus is lifted up (His death on the cross), He will drag me to my redemption. Jesus' being lifted up on the cross must not only be a historical event of some two thousands years ago, it must be my daily experience. It has been revealed that I must experience my dying off daily by His death on the cross. As Paul wrote to the Romans:

What shall we say then? Shall we continue in sin, that grace may abound? God forbid. How shall we, that are dead to sin, live any longer therein? Know ye not, that so many of us as were baptized into Jesus Christ were baptized into his death? Therefore we are buried with him by baptism into death: that like as Christ was raised up from the dead by the glory of the Father, even so we also should walk in newness of life. For if we have been planted together in the likeness of his death, we shall be also in the likeness of his resurrection: Knowing this, that our old man is crucified with him, that the body of sin might be destroyed, that henceforth we should not serve sin. For he that is dead is freed from sin. Now if we be dead with Christ, we believe that we shall also live with him: Knowing that Christ being raised from the dead dieth no more; death hath no more dominion over him. For in that he died, he died unto sin once: but in that he liveth, he liveth unto God. Likewise reckon ye also yourselves to be dead indeed unto sin, but alive unto God through Jesus Christ our Lord. Let not sin therefore reign in your mortal body, that ye should obey it in the lusts thereof. Neither yield ye your members as instruments of unrighteousness unto sin: but yield yourselves unto God, as those that are alive from the dead and your members as instruments of righteousness unto God. For sin shall not have dominion over you: for ye are not under the law, but under grace (6:1–14).

For me to experience this new life in Christ continually, I must understand this "tale of death," contained in this powerful revelation of the mysteries of grace.

Paul emphasized my need to experience the death of Jesus Christ continually by his usage of the words *dead*, *dieth*, and *death* in verse nine: "Knowing that Christ being raised from the dead dieth no more; death hath no more dominion over him." Sadly, most English-speaking people interpret the words *dead*, *dieth*, and *death* to mean the same thing. Each of them has a far-reaching different definition, however. For example, "Knowing that Christ being raised from the dead [meaning "a corpse"] dieth [meaning "to die off"] no more; death [meaning "to die"] hath no more dominion over him."

Now I realize that all my struggles have occurred because I did not understand the meaning of the death and resurrection of Jesus Christ for my life.

What shall we say then? Shall we continue in sin, that grace may abound? God forbid. How shall we, that are dead {to die off} to sin, live any longer therein? Know ye not, that so many of us as were baptized into Jesus Christ were baptized into his death {to die}? Therefore we are buried with him by baptism into death {to die}: that like as Christ was raised up from the dead {a corpse} by the glory of the Father, even so we also should walk in newness of life. For if we have been planted together in the likeness of his death {to die}, we shall be also in the likeness of his resurrection: Knowing this, that our old man is crucified with him, that the body of sin might be destroyed, that henceforth we should not serve sin. For he that is dead {to die off} is freed from sin. Now if we be dead {to die off} with Christ, we believe that we shall also live with him: Knowing that Christ being raised from the dead {a corpse} dieth {to die off} no more; death {to die} hath no more dominion over him. For in that he died {to die off}, he died {to die off} unto sin once: but in that he liveth, he liveth unto God. Likewise reckon ye also yourselves to be dead {a corpse} indeed unto sin, but alive unto God through Jesus Christ our Lord. Let not sin therefore reign in your mortal body, that ye should obey it in the lusts thereof. Neither yield ye your members as instruments of unrighteousness unto sin: but yield yourselves unto God, as those that are alive from the dead {a corpse} and your members as instruments of righteousness unto God. For sin shall not have dominion over you: for ye are not under the law, but under grace (6:1–14).

I never understood that the word *death*, meaning "to die," is associated only with Jesus. It is never used in conjunction with the believer. Oh, how I have tried to live the crucified life. I tried to live life as if I was actually dead. What futility! Only Jesus has died and been raised from the dead to live the resurrected life.

I did not know that experiencing my death occurs only in His death as I continually experience my "dying off." My dying off is not a one-time occurrence. It must be a continual, daily occurrence.

Now, I understand I will never experience the death of "to die" until I experience the grave. Thanks be to Jesus Christ, however, I can experience my continual dying off in this life by the grace of God, by being "baptized into Jesus Christ" (Rom. 6:3). The continual life of Jesus is made manifest in my mortal body, but only if my life is never attempted in my mortal body, in my self-centeredness. I am alive but dying, yet dying I live. It is a mystery, but continual life is only experienced in the continual death (dying off) of my own flesh:

Always bearing about in the body the dying of the Lord Jesus, that the life also of Jesus might be made manifest in our body. For we which live are alway{s} delivered unto death for Jesus' sake, that the life also of Jesus might be made manifest in our mortal flesh (2 Cor. 4:10–11).

The good news, the Gospel, has declared that the Father has sent His Son into my world to baptize me with His Holy Spirit that my "mortality might be swallowed up of life" (2 Cor. 5:4).

If Jesus will continually be lifted up (John 12:32), if I can continually hear Him (John 6:63), if the Word can continually be set with my heart (Matt. 13:18–23), I will finally arrive at my destiny, complete oneness with Jesus Christ. I will come to know what it means to be filled with the Spirit. I will come to know what it means to be spiritual.

The continual lifting up of Jesus in my life eventually "drags" me into submission to the Spirit. I know I will get there, but I also know "another shall gird [me], and carry [me] whither [I] wouldest not [go]" (John 21:18). Since my hope is Jesus and not my effort, I know I will arrive. Yet, I also know I will arrive, resisting it with every fiber of my self-centeredness.

This series of books contains the story of my resistance. If it were not for that resistance, this narrative would be a much fuller revelation of the sovereign power of God. Thus it is an account of the author's struggle to be saved from himself, the story of one man coming to grips with Jesus Christ as the Way.

My resistance, moreover, makes this story incomplete. It is only the sharing of the revelation of Jesus Christ as I have experienced it. I have tried to tell the story as it unfolded to me. Therefore, the first volume may seem to be elementary, but it is, in part, my early struggles with the grace of God. My hope is that the journey will be completed.

chapter 1

Challenge of Grace

A young child overhears his mother and father fighting in another room. Parents learn their teenage daughter is pregnant. A sleepless, worried mother finally hears her son coming home, but he is intoxicated again. A confused, lonely husband struggles to understand how his marriage ended. Fear, hurt, and pain grip the lives of far too many people who find themselves confronting this thing called life. People desperately wanting to live, needing to live, yet seemingly, always thwarted from living by life itself.

Many forge ahead, trying to catch their "moment in the sun," only to find, even if they catch the elusive dream, the moment is lacking. They set out to make it to the top of the mountain, only to find that as they near the top, some unforeseen figure or event knocks them back into the valley. Sadly, their life is spent in a seemingly endless search for meaning, fulfillment, and satisfaction. In desperation, they wonder what is wrong with their lives.

Unfortunately, many believers experience the same struggles as unbelievers. Most believers state that Christianity is abundant life, but they just never seem to experience it. Or, if they do, it seems to be either fleeting or of short duration. Failing to understand the very heartbeat of Christianity, far too many believers never seem to get on top of their circumstances.

Many contributing factors cause people to struggle in life. One reason stands out above any of the others, however. Far too many people can't cope with the common pressures of daily living. Circumstances, often beyond their control, close in on them, restricting their movement, and prohibiting them from holding up under the pressures. In the midst of troubles, perplexities, endless persecutions, and being cast down, they have a strong sense of distress, despair, being forsaken and destroyed.

In far too many instances, nonbelievers, as well as many believers, can't find freedom from the pressure. They cannot flee for refuge. They do not have an anchor in life that holds them "sure and steadfast" (Heb. 16:19) in the midst of the storms. Having no hope to sustain them, they do not experience the "peace of God that passeth all understanding" (Phil. 4:7). They flounder upon the sea of life and are tossed to and fro with every wind and wave of adversity. They need deliverance from the overbearing circumstances of life. They need salvation.

Jesus Christ: In Him We Live

There is good news! The gospel of Jesus Christ proclaims there is hope. The Word of God boldly declares that the grace of God is sufficient to produce peace in the midst of perilous times. The author of the book of Hebrews wrote:

Wherein God, willing more abundantly to show unto the heirs of promise the immutability of his counsel, confirmed it by an oath: That by two immutable things, in which it was impossible for God to lie, we might have a strong consolation, who have fled for refuge to lay hold upon the hope set before us: Which hope we have as an anchor of the soul, both sure and steadfast, and which entereth into that within the veil; Whither the forerunner is for us entered, even Jesus, made an high priest for ever after the order of Melchizedek (Heb. 6:17–20).

Perilous times. The letter of Hebrews was probably written to second-generation believers. Their parents were probably the first ones in Rome to accept Jesus Christ as their Savior. Consequently, many of their parents had died in the midst of the great persecutions that followed. The apparent resurgence of persecution brought this generation face to face with the same threatening fires of death. They also found themselves in perilous times.

Spiritual problem. Even more dangerous than the persecutions and the agonizing threat of death, however, was the fact that they faced a very serious spiritual problem. These Hebrew Christians had been converted from Judaism, but evidently they were beginning to lose the vitality of their new spiritual experience. They were tempted to forsake Jesus Christ as their Messiah and to slip back into Judaism. They returned to some of their old ways, and the fires of persecution probably hastened the backsliding process.

The Epistle of Hebrews encouraged them to continue their acceptance of Jesus Christ. It was written to show them that Jesus Christ was far better than anything they had left behind in Judaism. It revealed that Jesus Christ, regardless of the kind of trouble the readers would face, is the answer for peace, joy, and abundant life.

HOPE FOR MAN. The Epistle of Hebrews was written to confirm the mystery of life, "which hath been hid from ages and from generations, but now is made manifest to [all believers]" (Col. 1:26). The writer of Hebrews wanted the readers of his letter to understand this secret of life. He wanted them to know ". . . God would make known what is the riches of the glory of this mystery . . . which is Christ in you, the hope of glory" (Col. 1:27). He wanted them to know Jesus Christ is the only hope for man.

Jesus Christ: City of refuge. The writer of Hebrews told those early Christians that they could have hope in their troubles if they would only flee for refuge". This probably referred to the cities of refuge in the Old Testament (Num. 35), a concept they knew and understood. When someone was in trouble, in the old "eye for an eye, tooth for a tooth" system of justice (Exod. 21:24), he could escape to one of several cities of refuge and be safe from the avenger. The troubled Christians in the first century could also escape, if they would only flee for refuge.

As long as the early Christians remained within the "walls" of Jesus Christ, they had a hope that the score could be settled without unmerciful revenge. Christians of every generation need to understand they have a city of refuge from troubling circumstances. Every believer must come to understand what it means to be "in Him."

Jesus Christ: Anchor. Jesus Christ, as the believer's city of refuge, is the great hope. "Which hope we have as an anchor of the soul, both sure and steadfast, and which entereth into that within the veil" (Heb. 6:19). Jesus Christ can stabilize every life in the midst of storms for He, as the "forerunner" (Heb. 6:20), is a hope that is "sure and steadfast." The anchor will hold. It will hold because Jesus Christ has "entereth into that within the veil" (Heb. 6:19–20). He has done what no man can do. He has passed from without the veil to within the veil. Jesus Christ has passed from death to life.

In the death, resurrection, and ascension of Jesus Christ, the veil was rent for all mankind. In crossing the great chasm that separated God and man, Jesus made the reconciliation of man to God possible. He became the forerunner, so that all men might go where they could not go before, into the heavenly realm. Jesus Christ, the anchor, is both "sure and steadfast," because He has crossed the chasm from earth to heaven, from flesh to Spirit, and from death to life. Jesus Christ is the anchor that stabilizes man. He produces the heavenly, the spiritual, and life itself in earthly, fleshly, and dying man. In Him, man can experience life.

Jesus Christ: Fortress of hope. The believer himself can now enter into the heavenly holy of holies because of his oneness with Jesus Christ, the heavenly high priest. Being in Christ produces a marvelous fortress of hope:

> *. . . a strong consolation, who have fled for refuge to lay hold upon the hope set before us: Which hope we have as an anchor of the soul, sure and steadfast, and which entereth into that within the veil* (Heb. 6:18–19).

The hope the believer has in Jesus Christ is not a faint glimmer of light at the end of the tunnel. It is a fortress of hope, "a strong consolation." The believer can face the challenges of life because he has a city of refuge. He has an anchor that holds. He has a source of life that has already accomplished all that the believer desires to pass from death to life. The believer in Jesus Christ has a fortress of hope.

There is no trouble, no storm, nor disaster that cannot be conquered by the grace of God. Deliverance from every overbearing circumstance can be experienced because He has already been delivered from them. He is an anchor that can calm the soul in the midst of the storms. He is the city of refuge. Within the "walls" of Jesus Christ, there is life.

Jesus Christ: In Him We Move

Moreover, the believer can continually experience this life of Jesus. When the believer "moves" in Jesus, he moves through life with grace. For example, several occurrences in the life of Paul reveal the grace of God at work in perilous times.

Paul neared the end of his third missionary journey, and according to scholars, he probably resided briefly at Corinth during A.D. 57 or 58. The collection of relief aid for the poverty-stricken believers in Jerusalem had been gathered. He was preparing to take the aid to Jerusalem (Acts 29:22).

In this milieu, Paul wrote his letter to the Roman saints. In the introduction, Paul prayed for a prosperous journey: "Making request, if by any means now at length I might have a prosperous journey by the will of God to come unto you" (Rom. 1:10).

The prayer seemed harmless enough. It simply expressed Paul's desire to carry the gospel message to Rome. The short phrase, "by any means," in that prayer eventually revealed the depths of Paul's understanding of grace. The will of God would be accomplished. Paul would get to Rome, but what a journey.

PAUL'S JOURNEY. After Paul prayed for a prosperous journey to Rome, the prophet Agabus came to Paul with a challenging word from the Lord. Agabus specifically prophesied that Paul would be placed in bonds and delivered ". . . into the hands of the Gentiles" (Acts 21:11). Paul would get to Rome, but he would go as a prisoner.

Plagued. Moreover, his journey was plagued with events that would cause most Christians today to wonder if it were indeed God's will for Paul to go to Rome. Within the first twelve days after entering Jerusalem, Paul experienced the following adversities: ". . . the Jews . . . stirred up all the people, and laid hands on him . . . and drew him out of the temple . . ." (Act 21:27, 30); the Jews intended to kill him by beating him to death (21:31–32); he was "bound with . . . chains" (21:33); he was mistaken for an Egyptian who was responsible for a band of four thousand murderers (21:38); Roman soldiers "bound him with thongs" (22:25), intending to "scourge" him (22:24); more than forty ". . . Jews banded together, and bound themselves under a curse, saying that they would neither eat nor drink till they had killed Paul" (23:12–13). Needless to say, it seemed that Paul had a rough two weeks when he first arrived in Jerusalem. Remember, God was answering his prayer for a "prosperous journey" to Rome.

Perils at sea. Paul spent the next two years "in bonds" (Acts 24:27), struggling with the charges and counter-charges of the Jews. After having to undergo the ". . . many and grievous complaints against [him] . . ."

(25:7) by the Jews, he survived a severe storm at sea for many days (27:9–28). Moreover, Paul had to live through a shipwreck (27:29–44) and the bite of a venomous viper (28:1–6) before he arrived at his destination.

Prisoner of Rome. Finally, even after arriving at Rome, he remained under house arrest, chained to a Roman soldier for two years (Acts 28:16–17, 20, 30). Evidently, when he first arrived in Rome, "no man stood with him, but all men forsook [him] . . ." (2 Tim. 4:16). While a prisoner, some of his own "brethren" preached "Christ of contention, not sincerely, supposing to add affliction to [his] bonds" (Phil. 1:16).

PAUL'S PROSPERITY. The perils of Paul on his journey to Rome would probably have most Christians wondering why God had forsaken them. Yet Paul seemed to accept them as just part of his journey to fulfill the will of God. He understood that being a "prisoner of Rome" was God's means for his arrival and ministry in Rome. Amazingly, he never considered himself to be a prisoner of Rome but a prisoner of the Lord (Eph. 4:1).

Source. Paul knew that this treasure of the gospel of Jesus Christ was in "earthen vessels, that the excellency of the power may be of God, and not of [him]" (2 Cor. 4:7). He knew that God was well able to fulfill His purpose, no matter what happened to him. Paul could say, "We are troubled on every side, yet not distressed; we are perplexed, but not in despair; persecuted, but not forsaken; cast down, but not destroyed" (2 Cor. 4:8). He could proclaim, ". . . by the grace of God I am what I am: and his grace which was bestowed upon me was not in vain; but I laboured more abundantly than they all: yet not I, but the grace of God which was with me" (1 Cor. 15:10).

Life. In another letter written while in prison, Paul wrote: "For the which cause [the ministry] I also suffer these things: nevertheless I am not ashamed: for I know whom I have believed, and am persuaded that he is able to keep that which I have committed [the ministry] unto him against that day" (2 Tim. 1:12). Paul wrote in the same letter, "Wherein I suffer trouble, as an evildoer, even unto bonds; but the word of God is not bound" (2:9).

Finally, he wrote to the Philippians a remarkable testimony of the grace of God at work in his life. He stated, "Yea, and if I be offered upon the sacrifice and service of your faith, I joy, and rejoice with you all" (Phil. 2:17). He rejoiced in the opportunity to experience God in the sacrifice of his life. Paul experienced the prosperity of a joyful life in the midst of perilous times.

Conclusion. Paul resounded with a mighty "Now unto the King eternal, immortal, invisible, the only wise God, be honour and glory for ever and ever . . ." (1 Tim. 1:17). How could he write this? He knew that for true prosperity, life does not hinge upon the circumstances. He stated to the Philippians:

> *But I would ye should understand, brethren, that the things which happened unto me have fallen out rather unto the furtherance of the gospel; So that my bonds in Christ are manifest in all the palace, and in all other places; And many of the brethren in the Lord, waxing confident by my bonds, are much more bold to speak the word without fear. Some indeed preach Christ even of envy and strife; and some also of good will: The one preach Christ of contention, not sincerely, supposing to add affliction to my bonds: But the other of love, knowing that I am set for the defense of the gospel. What then? notwithstanding, every way, whether in pretense, or in truth, Christ is preached; and I therein do rejoice, yea, and will rejoice* (Phil. 1:12–18).

Because Paul moved in Christ, he moved through life in grace.

Jesus Christ: In Him We Have Our Being

In Paul's letter to the Ephesian saints, he described the characteristics of this grace-filled life that enabled him to rejoice in perilous times. He described what it means to have Jesus as the essence of his being:

And be not drunk with wine, wherein is excess; but be filled with the Spirit; Speaking to yourselves in psalms and hymns and spiritual songs, singing and making melody in your heart to the Lord; Giving thanks always for all things unto God and the Father in the name of our Lord Jesus Christ; Submitting yourselves one to another in the fear of God (Eph. 5:18–21).

In one sentence, Paul gave the evidence of being "baptized with the Holy Spirit," the evidence of living by grace.

FILLED WITH THE SPIRIT. The Christian, being "filled with the Spirit," manifests three characteristics. He will be "speaking to [himself] in psalms and hymns and spiritual songs, singing and making melody in [his] heart to the Lord." He will be "giving thanks always for all things unto God and the Father in the name of our Lord Jesus Christ." Finally, he will be "submitting [himself] one to another in the fear of the Lord." The Spirited-filled Christian, one who has Jesus as the essence of his being, will have a joyful heart, a thankful attitude, and a submissive will.

Joyful heart. "Speaking to [one's self] in psalms and hymns and spiritual songs, singing and making melody in [the] heart to the Lord" can only come out of a heart that has its being in Jesus. While happiness (that which is derived from "happenings") rises and falls with the events of life, joy is solid and steadfast in the midst of changing circumstances. Joy is experienced because life is not in the outward circumstances, but in the inner essence of Jesus in the heart.

Joy is a cheerfulness that arises out of a sense of being "calmly well-off" in Jesus. It is delighting in the Lord as the essence of life as opposed to the attempt to delight in the happenings of life itself. It is produced only by the Spirit and permeates the believer to the point that Jesus is the "being" of the believer.

Thankful attitude. Likewise, "giving thanks always for all things unto God" is a reality only "in the name of our Lord Jesus Christ." No man anywhere (except Jesus) has the capability of producing thankfulness in situations that are not thankful. Only grace allows the capability to "glory in tribulations also: knowing that tribulation worketh patience" (Rom. 5:3). The grace-filled life can produce thankfulness in situations that are perilous, because the believer knows "all things work together for good. . . ." (8:28).

Thankfulness is not something the believer tries to produce, however. He does not try to be thankful when he is not thankful simply because the Scripture says to be thankful. The attribute of thankfulness is a product of the Spirit. If thankfulness is not there in trying times, then the Spirit is not in control. The only means of "giving thanks always for all things" is to have Jesus as the "being" of existence. In Him, there is thankfulness in every circumstance.

Submissive will. "Submitting yourselves one to another in the fear of the Lord" can only be produced by the free flow of the grace of God. Every man (except Jesus), because of the fear of loneliness, learns to modify his behavior toward others. In other words, man will sufficiently change his behavior in an attempt to receive what he thinks he needs from others. Therefore, man submits to others only as long as he perceives he will get something out of it. Since the fall, every man has learned to use other people rather than submit to them.

Only the gospel of Jesus Christ proclaims the reality that life is not in "using others," but it is in "living in others." Being a complete person is to experience Jesus in others. Only when the believer understands that the "being" of his life is "Jesus experienced in others" will there be a complete submitting to one another.

With Jesus Christ as the essence of man's being, there is always a joyful heart, a thankful attitude, and a submissive will. The evidence of a Spirit-filled life is the marvelous manifestation of Jesus in one's life, regardless of the circumstances. With Jesus Christ as his "being," man can move through life with grace. In Him, there is life.

CHALLENGE. Paul demonstrated this living in the Spirit when he wrote to the Corinthians: "We are troubled on every side, yet not distressed;

we are perplexed, but not in despair; persecuted, but not forsaken; cast down, but not destroyed. . . . For all things are for your sakes, that the abundant grace might . . . redound to the glory of God" (2 Cor. 4:8–9, 15). The circumstances of life did not dictate to Paul his quality of life. In spite of the perilous times, he experienced the "peace that passeth understanding." The grace of God always produces the joyful life.

Victorious living. Paul spoke of this victorious living to the Roman saints: "For if by one man's offence death reigned by one; much more they which receive abundance of grace and of the gift of righteousness shall reign in life by one, Jesus Christ" (Rom. 5:17). Jesus spoke of the grace-filled life: ". . . I am come that they might have life, and that they might have it more abundantly" (John 10:10). Jesus, the founder of Christianity, and Paul, perhaps its best spokesman, both proclaimed that the life of every believer should be victorious.

Frustrated living. Unfortunately, the reality of far too many Spirit-filled Christians is not one of victory, but rather of frustration, failure, and defeat. The Spirit-filled Christian often reacts to life much like the nonbeliever. When circumstances are good, life is good. When circumstances get tough, life is tough. The emotional roller coaster of far too many Christians rises and falls with their circumstances. Situations reign over the believer rather than the believer reigning over situations.

Grace of God. Why do so many believers experience failure and defeat when the promise of victory is so prevalent? The answer to that question lies in a statement that Paul made to the Galatian saints: "I am crucified with Christ; nevertheless I live; yet not I, but Christ liveth in me. . . . I do not frustrate the grace of God. . . ." (Gal. 2:20–21). Paul did not frustrate grace, and that "abundance of grace" enabled him to reign in life.

Circumstances, perceived to be good or bad, never indicate whether one is living the Spirit-filled life. It is, in fact, not the circumstances a person faces, but *how* he faces the circumstances that determines the accomplishment of the will of God. Amazingly, Paul, instead of being critical about the adversity he had to endure, took those potential calamities and, by the grace of God, turned them into greater opportunities for ministry. Instead of becoming the victim of the circumstances, he allowed God to use those circumstances in order to be the victor. The free flow of the grace of God is sufficient for every need in every time.

Because Paul's face was set upon the grace of God, his terrifying circumstances could not deter him. The will of God would be accomplished, not by deliverance out of the perils, but in the very midst of them. Christian prosperity has always been measured by the evidence of a joyful heart, a thankful attitude, and a submissive will in the believer. It has never been measured by the conditions that surround the believer. The joyful life is always determined by the flow of the grace of God and not by the materialistic circumstances of the surroundings: "For all things are for your sakes, that the abundant grace might through the thanksgiving of many redound to the glory of God" (2 Cor. 4:15); and "Wherein I suffer trouble, as an evil doer, even unto bonds; but the word of God is not bound. Therefore I endure all things for the elect's sakes, that they may also obtain the salvation which is in Christ Jesus with eternal glory" (2 Tim. 2:9–10).

May the experiences of Paul, one empowered by God, reveal the need for every Christian to experience greater heights of understanding the grace of God. May Jesus Christ, the city of refuge, become the realized fortress of hope. May every believer who struggles to experience "the peace that passeth understanding" come to experience the fullness of what it means to live the grace-filled life. May grace and peace be unto every believer in Jesus Christ.

Beginning of Grace

Jesus Christ is abundant life! He said, "The thief cometh not, but to steal and to kill, and to destroy: I am come that they might have life, and that they might have it more abundantly" (John 10:10). Jesus Christ came that all men might experience rich, full, glorious lives.

Paul described this abundant life as peace, preservation, joy, patience, character, hope, and love:

> *Therefore being justified by faith, we have peace with God through our Lord Jesus Christ: By whom also we have access by faith into this grace wherein we stand, and rejoice in hope of the glory of God. And not only so, but we glory in tribulations also: knowing that tribulation worketh patience; And patience, experience; and experience, hope: And hope maketh not ashamed; because the love of God is shed abroad in our hearts by the Holy Ghost which is given unto us.* (Rom. 5:1–5)

Because God's love can penetrate the heart of man, abundant life can be a reality for man. Moreover, nothing can separate man from God's love.

> *Who shall separate us from the love of Christ? shall trouble or hardship or persecution or famine or nakedness or danger or sword? As it is written, for thy sake we are killed all the day long; we are accounted as sheep for the slaughter. Nay, in all these things we are more than conquerors through him that loved us. For I am persuaded, that neither death, nor life, nor angels, nor principalities, nor powers nor things present, nor things to come, Nor height, nor depth, nor any other creature, shall be able to separate us from the love of God, which is in Christ Jesus our Lord* (Rom. 8:35–39.)

No circumstances can destroy the abundant life of Jesus. Experiencing this abundant life is a free gift by the grace of God. Peter stated, "Grace and peace be multiplied unto you through the knowledge of God, and of Jesus our Lord, According as his divine power hath given unto us all things that pertain unto life. . . ." (2 Pet. 1:2–3). Paul emphasized the freeness of the whole plan of salvation when he wrote, "For by grace are ye saved through faith; and that not of yourselves: it is the gift of God: Not of works, lest any man should boast" (Eph. 2:8–9). Through the death and resurrection of Jesus Christ, all men can freely experience the abundant life that is in Him.

Jesus Christ is Life

Experiencing the joy of life can only be in Jesus Christ. It is not attempting to live life in life itself, or even to attempt to live for Jesus. It is to live *in* Him.

Writing to a group of people struggling with this issue of living life in Him, Paul stated, "My little children, of whom I travail in birth again until Christ be formed in you" (Gal. 4:19). Something had occurred that robbed them of the abundant life they once experienced. Although Paul did not tell them directly in this verse what took away their abundant life, he did tell them what would cure their problem. He would travail again "until Christ [would] be formed in [them]."

A more literal translation of that statement is "until the mind and life in complete harmony with Christ shall have been formed in you." Paul defined for them what it means to live: having Christ formed in them or being in the process of having Christ formed in them. Since Jesus Christ is life, each individual must be formed in Him in order to experience life.

FORMING OF CHRIST. The real question is: "How is Christ formed in the life of the Christian?" The phrase "be formed" is a verb in the passive voice. In the passive voice, the subject is acted upon. Thus, the subject, Christ, is being acted upon by someone, which, in turn, produces the correct outward expression in the believer.

In other words, what process causes the individual (who has Christ on the inside) to become such a person in whom the world can see Christ on the outside? The answer to that question is the answer to the secret of life. It is the understanding of the mysteries of the grace of God.

How is Christ formed in the believer? Many believe and preach that Christlikeness is formed by imitation. They study the Bible to find out what a Christian must do. Then they attempt to do those "imperative commands," by living for Christ. Their understanding is that to be Christlike, they must imitate Christ in the things He did.

Sadly, however, this is self-righteousness. It always comes up short. It constantly produces a life-style in which those who attempt to imitate Christ in His actions "cannot do the things that [they] would" (Gal. 5:17). The reality of their life always seems to fall far short of their expectations.

Transformation. How do believers have Christ formed in them? Paul, in his letter to the Romans, proclaimed, "And be not conformed to this world: but be ye transformed by the renewing of your mind. . . ." (Rom. 12:2). The key word in Paul's statement is *transformed*. The Christian is not to be like the world, but he is to be transformed. Hidden in this word, *transformed*, is the real essence of what it means to have Christ formed in the believer. Christ being formed in an individual will transform the individual.

In the Mount of Transfiguration experience of Jesus, we find the same word used by Paul to the Roman saints, except it is translated "transfigured." Jesus "was transfigured before them: and his face did shine as the sun, and his raiment was white as the light" (Matt. 17:2). Paul wanted the Galatian saints to have Christ formed in them. He wanted the Roman saints to be transformed. Jesus was transfigured.

Before the transfiguration on the mountain, Peter, James, and John saw the outward appearance of Jesus to be as any other human being. When Jesus was transfigured, however, they saw Him (to the limit that man can see God) as He really was, the Son of God. The essence of what Jesus was on the inside shone through to the outside. He was transfigured.

In Paul's statement to the Romans, he says that all believers should become transfigured, transformed saints. They should not be like the world, but they should let that which they really are on the inside, shine through to be formed on the outside. The world should see them as they really are, Christians.

Paul desired this for the Galatian saints. He knew they had Christ within them, but he wanted Christ to be seen in their lives. He wanted them to understand that what it means to be Christian is to have Jesus Christ on the inside, working on the outside. The world should see Jesus Christ in the lives of all Christians.

Changed by the Holy Spirit. Obviously, Jesus being transfigured, and Paul's admonition for the Romans to "be ye transformed", are similar statements. They still do not reveal the process of that transformation; the process of having Christ formed in the believer, however. The means of the transformation is revealed in the only other place where the Greek word translated "transformed" in Romans 12 and "transfigured" in Matthew 17 is found in the New Testament: 2 Corinthians 3:18.

Paul wrote to the Corinthians: "But we all . . . are changed into the same image from glory to glory, even as by the Spirit of the Lord" (2 Cor. 3:18). The phrase "are changed" is the same word translated as "transformed" and "transfigured." Here, however, Paul gave added insight to the process of becoming a transfigured saint; the process of having Christ formed in the believer: "even as by the Spirit of the Lord."

Transformation by participation. Again in Paul's statement to the Galatians, "Christ be formed in you," the verb is a passive verb. Something acts upon the subject to produce the proper outward manifestation in the believer. The believer is to become a transfigured saint by the production of the Holy Spirit. Christlikeness is not by the imitation of Christ but by the participation of being in Christ.

Christians are to imitate Christ only in how He did the will of the Father. Jesus said, ". . . the Father that dwelleth in me, he doeth the work" (John 14:10). The Father, through the Holy Spirit, worked His will in, and through, His Son. In all that Christ did, it was the Father in Him doing the work. The Son did not let the Father help him do the work. The Father did the work Himself, in and through the Son.

The believer is transformed in the same manner as work was accomplished in the life of Christ. Christ being formed in the believer is not by works of the believer but by the works of the Holy Spirit. The works (of the believer) for Christ only produce death, but the production of the Holy Spirit in the believer who is in Christ, produces abundant, victorious life. The key to becoming a transformed saint is allowing the Holy Spirit liberty to perform the work of Christ in the believer. The emphasis must always be on *being* a Christian rather than *doing* as a Christian should do.

DILUTED GOSPEL. In Galatians 4:19, Paul implied that something had happened to these saints. He stated that he must travail once again for them. The struggle that the Galatian saints found themselves facing again is the continual struggle that occurs when Jesus is not the sole emphasis of life.

Perversion. Something had happened to the Christians in Galatia. Paul wrote to them, "Ye did run well; who did hinder you. . . . " (Gal. 5:7). He added, ". . . Who hath bewitched you, that ye should not obey the truth, before whose eyes Jesus Christ hath been evidently set forth. . . . " (Gal. 3:1). He proclaimed, "I marvel that ye are so soon removed from him . . . [to a perverted] gospel of Christ" (Gal. 1:6–7). Paul wanted to know who was responsible for their eyes being taken off Jesus. More importantly, why were they removed? He still considered them to be Christians, but he knew they were not experiencing the abundant life of liberty and freedom in Christ (Gal. 5:1).

The Christians in the churches of Galatia had been won to Christ in Paul's first missionary journey. They had readily accepted the gospel. After Paul departed, certain Christian teachers, who were probably Christians converted out of Judaism, came to Galatia and began to teach (Gal. 2:12–15). Evidently, these teachers were instrumental in turning the eyes of the Galatian saints off Jesus and onto something else. Whatever they were teaching the Galatians, it was killing them: "so that [they could not] do the things that [they] would" (Gal. 5:17).

Works of the Law. A clue to what these teachers from Jerusalem were teaching can be found in the phrase, "works of the law," a phrase Paul used six times in the first three chapters of Galatians. Although the entire letter to the Galatians was written because of this misunderstanding of the works of the law, in Paul's letter to the Romans, he illustrated the truth more clearly. He wrote:

> *Know ye not, brethren, (for I speak to them that know the law,) how that the law hath dominion over a man as long as he liveth? For the woman which hath an husband is bound by the law to her husband so long as he liveth; but if the husband be dead, she is loosed from the law of her husband. So then if, while her husband liveth, she be married to another man, she shall be called an adulteress: but if her husband be dead, she is free from that law; So that she is no adulteress, though she be married to another man* (Rom. 7:1–3).

After stating the above truth, Paul then revealed why he used this analogy of husband and wife. He stated:

Wherefore, my brethren, ye also are become dead to the law by the body of Christ; that ye should be married to another, even to him who is raised from the dead, that we should bring forth fruit unto God. For when we were in the flesh, the motions of sins, which were by the law, did work in our members to bring forth fruit unto death. But now we are delivered from the law, that being dead wherein we were held; that we should serve in newness of the spirit, and not in the oldness of the letter (Rom. 7:4–6).

In this passage to the Romans, Paul revealed what he called a perverted gospel in his letter to the Galatians (Gal. 1:7). It is also the revelation of that which causes the Christian to struggle. It is the attempt to live "by the law."

Adulterated gospel. All men must become dead to their own self-effort to experience life and become "married" to Christ. It is the continuing struggle of what or who is the source of living. The worldly person lives for himself through himself. The religious person lives for God through himself. The true Christian lives through Christ.

The true believer experiences life because he allows Christ, who is the only source of life, the liberty to *be* life for and in Him. The pure gospel of Jesus Christ proclaims that Jesus, and Jesus alone, is the source of life. All men can experience life only by being in Christ.

An adulterated gospel proclaims that life is Jesus plus something else, however. Sadly, this adulterated gospel only produces a life-style "so that [the Christian or the unbeliever] cannot do the things that [he] would" (Gal. 5:17). How sad to have Jesus Christ living within the believer but to no effect (5:4); to have Christ actually dwelling within the Christian, but Christ profiting the Christian nothing (5:2). The Holy Spirit actually desires to transform the believer into a transfigured saint of God but is thwarted, quenched, and frustrated by the believer's desire to be righteous or to live by his own works.

If Christians believe Jesus died for their sins to be forgiven, why is it so hard for most to believe that Jesus was raised from the dead to live the Christian life for them? Paul said to the Galatians, "I marvel that ye are so soon removed from him that called you into the grace of Christ unto another gospel: Which is not another; but there be some that trouble you, and would pervert the gospel of Christ" (1:6–7). This perverted gospel was not only the struggle of the church at Galatia but, sadly, it is the struggle of far too many Christians today.

Grace of God

The answer for the dilemma of the struggling Christian is an understanding of what it means to be Christian. Paul stated that those who had received "abundance of grace . . . shall reign in life by one, Jesus Christ" (Rom. 5:17). Without question, the grace of God is probably the most crucial issue of Christianity today. The struggling Christian, indeed all men who desire to experience life, must experience the free flow of God's grace. The reality of Peter's prayer, "But grow in grace, and in the knowledge of our Lord and Saviour Jesus Christ. . . ." (2 Pet. 3:18), must become a reality in the life of those who are not experiencing abundant life.

UNDERSTANDING GRACE. The original word from which *grace* is translated occurs over 160 times in the New Testament and is rendered *grace* 130 times. The oldest root meaning of the word translated *grace* carried the idea of sweetness or attractiveness. It later evolved into meaning "favor, goodwill, or loving kindness," especially when it related to the action of a king/subject or master/slave relationship. In the Old Testament, it was primarily used to describe God's favor to man. In the New Testament, it was developed one step further to indicate the favor of God toward man that is unearned or undeserved. It ultimately relates to the death and resurrection of Jesus Christ, which enables man to experience abundant life.

Grace equals labor. What does grace actually mean for daily living? Paul wrote, "But by the grace of God I am what I am. . . . I laboured more abundantly than they all: yet not I, but the grace of God which was with me" (1 Cor. 15:10). Paul's simple statement indicated that his labor was not of himself, but the labor seen in his life was by the grace of God. Labor does occur, but it is a product of grace.

Grace equals His working. The same principle is also stated to the Colossians; however, it is stated in a different way which adds insight to the meaning of grace. He wrote, "Whereunto I also labour, striving according to his working, which worketh in me mightily" (Col. 1:29). As indicated, labor is again being performed, but it is not Paul's labor. The labor Paul was experiencing was "according to [God's] working."

To the Corinthians, the apostle stated his labor was by the grace of God. To the Colossians, Paul stated his labor was by "[the Spirit's] working." In both statements, Paul proclaimed that labor was occurring. In one, however, labor is coupled with grace. In the other, it is correlated to the Holy Spirit. Obviously, then, the grace of God and the working of the Holy Spirit are connected.

Grace equals God doing His will. Finally, Paul helps our understanding of grace to come together by making a similar statement to the Philippians. He wrote, "For it is God which worketh in you both to will and to do of his good pleasure" (Phil. 2:13). It can be safely stated that "his good pleasure" can be understood as the doing of the will of God. Something that would be pleasurable to God would be His will. Thus, the verse could be interpreted to read, "For it is God which worketh in you both to will and to do His will."

In true Christianity, it is God who is active (literal meaning of "worketh") in the believer, who produces the will of God. In the final analysis, only God Himself can do His will. Both the "to will" and the "to do" of God's will are done by God Himself.

DEFINING GRACE. Just as Paul stated to the Corinthians and to the Colossians, he repeated to the Philippians, that it is God who does the work and not the believer. Based upon an application of Philippians 2:13, the specific work that God does in the believer is twofold. First Paul says, "It is God which worketh in you . . . to will . . ." The "to will" or the "want to" of the believer is a work of God Himself.

Desire to work for God. Admittedly, most believers attempt, or someone else attempts, to create a desire within themselves for the things of God. Only God can create that "want to," however. In fact, the revelation of God makes that very statement as Paul tells us in his letter to the Romans: "So then it is not of him that willeth . . . but of God that sheweth mercy" (Rom. 9:16).

No amount of human effort can create the desire to cause an individual to want to accomplish the will of God. The motivators and manipulators who try to stir man into action may get an initial response. The end result, however, will always be the same: "so that ye cannot do the things that ye would."

Peter's life illustrated this dilemma of man's effort to commitment. Peter said: ". . . Lord . . . I will lay down my life for thy sake." Jesus responded, "Wilt thou lay down thy life for my sake? Verily, verily, I say unto thee, The cock shall not crow, till thou hast denied me thrice" (John 13:37–38). A few hours later, Peter was not willing to give his life but denied Jesus three times (John 18:25–27). Eventually, Peter would experience his death, but it was not a work of Peter. It was the work of the Holy Spirit: ". . . thou shalt stretch forth thy hands, and another shall gird thee, and carry thee whither thou wouldest not" (John 21:18).

Man may be able to "will it" to a small degree; however, he does not have the capability to commit to the ultimate. All the Christian hype in the world cannot produce the "want to" that is necessary for the accomplishment of the will of God. Regardless of how much someone may incite, push, pull, beg, plead, or condemn with guilt, the "want to," the "will to," or the "desire" that is necessary for Christians to experience the will of God cannot be fabricated by human effort. The "want to" that all believers want to have is not a creation of the believer. It is produced by the grace of God.

Ability to do God's will. Likewise, God also gives the "to do" of His will. The ability that is necessary for the will of God to be accomplished is, again, a work of God Himself. No amount of effort put forth by man can do the ultimate will of God.

Paul again revealed this truth in his letter to the Romans: "So then it is not of him that willeth, nor of him that runneth, but of God that sheweth mercy" (9:16). Regardless of how many times believers are admonished for greater acts of determination and effort, it is not "of him that runneth," but of God who works in man to do His will.

Although man himself cannot do the will of God, the will of God can be seen in man's life. The will of God and the ability to do it is produced by God Himself. This ability, produced by God, is the actual essence of what it means to be Christian.

A working definition of grace. Now a working definition for the grace of God can be formulated. Building upon Paul's statements to the Corinthians, the Colossians, and the Philippians, the grace of God can be stated as "the want to and the accomplishment of the will of God" in a believer's life. Grace is the divine provision that God gives to His creation to enable it to fulfill its intended purpose.

Paul stated to the Corinthians, "I laboured more abundantly than they all: yet not I, but the grace of God." Paul labored but by the grace of God. He wrote to the Colossians, "Whereunto I also labour, striving according to his working." Paul labored, but it was according to the Holy Spirit's working. Thus the grace of God is the Spirit's working. Finally, Paul wrote to the Philippians, "For it is God which worketh in you both to will and to do of his good pleasure." The grace of God is the Spirit's working, and the Spirit's working is the "to will" and the "to do" of the will of God. Consequently, the grace of God is the want to and the accomplishment of the will of God. The grace of God is supernatural enablement!

This fundamental principle can be seen in another statement by Paul. He wrote to the Galatians concerning his ministry, "(For he that wrought effectually in Peter to the apostleship of the circumcision, the same was mighty in me toward the Gentiles)" (Gal.2:8). He then added, "And when James, Cephas, and John, who seemed to be pillars, perceived the grace that was given unto me, they gave to me and Barnabas the right hands of fellowship. . . ." (Gal. 2:9). Paul stated that grace is that which "wrought effectually" in both Peter and himself. *Grace is the provision by which God does His own will.*

The Spirit of God in every believer will not only produce the want to, but He will also produce the power to experience the Father's will, if He has but a yielded believer. All that God asks of any believer is to be only a channel through which He can flow to accomplish His own will. God's will on earth will be done, but it will be done as believers let Him work in them.

This fact is the amazing truth of what it means to be Christian. God reveals through His Word that He did not just send His Son to die on the cross for a sin penalty that man could be declared righteous. God also raised His Son from the dead to live within the believer that man could live righteously. Through the cross of Christ, man can be declared righteous, but equally important, through the resurrection of Christ, man has victory over sin for righteous living. By accepting Christ's death on the cross, man's sins can be forgiven. By letting the resurrected Christ live in him, man's life can be free from sin.

Jesus Christ is not only man's Savior; He is also man's life! The grace of God is the divine provision by which God enables man to live the life that God intended for him to live. The grace of God is divine enablement. Understanding its mysteries is to understand the secret of life.

Man's Oneness with Christ

Since the grace of God is clothed in mystery, man often rejects God's grace by his own attempt to live. Moreover, it seems that natural man does not want to be told that nothing within his power can affect the outcome of his eternal salvation (other than to reject Jesus Christ). Life is only within God.

Lying at the core of this struggle to understand the essence of life is the ever-present issue of law and grace. In the writings of Paul, the question was never "Should one be righteous?" Paul proclaimed that righteousness must be seen in everyone's life. The fact that righteousness was to be manifested was understood by all. How that righteousness was going to be produced, however, was a subject of much discussion.

For example, the meeting of the Jerusalem council tackled the law-or-grace issue. Many scholars feel that the underlying theme for most of Paul's letters to the various local congregations revolved around this issue. Most, if not all, of Paul's opponents in the first century opposed him on his revelation of grace.

THE REAL ISSUE OF LIFE. In Paul's letter to the Romans, the issue of law or grace revolved around the struggle of how righteousness was produced in the life of the believer. The question, "to be righteous or not to be righteous," was never raised. For example, the key word in Romans is *righteousness* (used over sixty times). The epistle's central theme is "How is that righteousness obtained?"

Paul seemed to have a unique understanding of how man was to experience the abundant life of Jesus. He implied the issue of life is actually a struggle over the "righteous issue." It is a struggle of good versus good, the source of life.

For example, it can be stated with reasonable certainty that Paul would never give permission for Christians even to struggle with acts of sin. According to Paul, if man struggles on the plane of "to sin [evil] or not to sin [good]," acts of sin always occur (Rom. 7). Why? Because acts of sin are not the problem. The struggle of life is never an issue of "good versus evil." They are the products of a deeper problem.

The struggle for abundant life must occur on a higher plane than good versus evil. If the Christian is to be victorious, he must be victorious over the initial struggle of "good versus good" (who is attempting to produce the good). The struggle of good versus good is the real issue of what it means to be Christian. It is a struggle to understand the mysteries of grace.

Struggle of God-like acts. Moreover, this struggle of good versus good is the heart of the gospel of Jesus Christ. Jesus' death on the cross is the means of man's salvation. Yet the cross is offensive to man (Gal. 5:11), because it proclaims man's inability to obtain righteousness in his own strength. Man continually struggles with the gospel's proclamation that he cannot produce his own salvation. Desperately desiring to produce good by himself, man gets trapped in the good-versus-good struggle.

Man, in the Garden of Eden, was tempted with the bait of becoming "as gods" (the source of good) before the commandment not to eat was broken and an act of sin occurred (Gen. 3:1–7). Man today, as epitomized by humanism, became his "own god" before the product of a godless society ever materialized (Rom. 1:17–32). Sadly, in the ranks of Christianity, many misguided Christians struggle with god-like acts long before acts of sin occur in their lives (Gal. 5:17–21). The misguided Christian attempts to be godly in his own strength, before he sees acts of sin happening in his life that he does not want to see.

The end product of all three examples is exactly the same. When an attempt is made to become as gods, to become one's own god, or to become more righteous by one's own god-likeness, acts of sin always occur. Acts of sin are always the product of attempting to be as gods, to become one's own god, and to "act as God." Acts of sin are the product of a deeper problem.

Realm of the struggle. To live the Christian life does require a struggle; however, the realm of that struggle must be understood if the believer is to be continually delivered. Many believers experience frustrations and even failure in their attempt to be Christian, simply because they do not comprehend the realm of the Christian warfare. They do not understand the good-versus-good issue.

What it means to be Christian basically implies that the individual is dead to himself, thereby allowing Christ to live within him. Paul stated it in this manner: "I am crucified with Christ: nevertheless I live; yet not I, but Christ liveth in me: and the life which I now live in the flesh I live by the faith of the Son of God, who loved me, and gave himself for me" (Gal. 2:20). The reality of being Christian means that the righteousness of God can be seen in an individual because He who is righteous lives through the individual.

If the professing Christian attempts to "do" righteousness in his own ability, however, sin always occurs because he has the treasure in an earthen vessel (2 Cor. 4:8). He is clothed with a body of flesh. He is flesh and his acts are always fleshly, producing sin. As Paul stated, "For I know that in me (that is, in my flesh,) dwelleth no good thing: for to will is present with me; but how to perform that which is good I find not" (Rom. 7:18).

It can be said that the Christian can live without sin because Christ lives within him. With the Christian not trying to live for God, Christ has freedom to live, and righteousness is produced in the life of the believer. Christ knows no sin, and where He lives there is righteousness. Understanding this truth moves the struggle of life from good versus evil to good versus good.

The problems always begin when the believer attempts to become godlike by his own efforts. If the believer attempts to do righteousness (doing right things, regardless of the motivation to do them: the Bible says to do them, the Church says to do them, or they are just the right things to do), then "Christ shall profit [the believer] nothing" (Gal. 5:2). "Christ is become of no effect unto [the believer]," because the individual attempts to do right by his own acts of righteousness (Gal. 5:4).

Danger of self-righteousness. Although some "perceived things" of righteousness may be done by the individual, the problem begins when he attempts to do those things in his own ability. If the believer attempts the perceived small things of righteousness, he becomes "debtor to do the whole law" (Gal. 5:3). The end result is as Paul stated concerning himself, "For that which I do I allow not: for what I would, that do I not; but what

I hate, that do I" (Rom. 7:15). Paul simply stated that within himself there is no hope of righteousness being performed in his life.

The believer "who walk[s] not after the flesh [in his own ability], but after the Spirit [the Christ within] . . . the righteousness of the law [will] be fulfilled in [the believer] . . ." (Rom. 8:1–4). The "hope of righteousness" is "through the Spirit" (Gal. 5:5). He who is righteousness is the only one who can live righteously. Therefore the believer must experience life by letting Jesus live.

JESUS CHRIST IS LIFE. The challenge for every believer is to realize where the struggle to be Christian actually occurs. The warfare is not good versus evil, which is the struggle of the moral man. The moral man may know what is good and what is evil. The Scripture proclaims that even though he knows good and evil, he is, however, incapable of always doing good and avoiding evil. In fact, if the struggle takes place on the level of good versus evil, evil always wins in the end, for man is a sinner by virtue of his natural birth.

The struggle for the Christian is warfare of good versus good. (Who does the good?) The first temptation that Satan throws before the Christian is the temptation to do good in the believer's own perceived ability. As stated previously, the misguided Christian struggles with god-like acts long before acts of sin occur in his life. Sin can be conquered, but it requires not only the death of Jesus, but also the resurrected Jesus to live within the believer. The believer lives because Jesus lives.

Warfare. If Christ does not have freedom to live within the believer, acts of sin eventually occur in the life of the Christian. Sin occurs because all men within their own essence are sinners. The apostle Paul recognized this fundamental truth when he wrote to Timothy, "This is a faithful saying, and worthy of all acceptation, that Christ Jesus came into the world to save sinners; of whom I am chief" (1 Tim. 1:15).

It is significant to point out that when Paul made this statement he had already experienced Jesus as his Savior. He had already established all the local churches that history records. He had already completed three missionary journeys. Within a few months of this statement, he wrote to Timothy: "I have fought a good fight, I have finished my course, I have kept the faith: henceforth there is laid up for me a crown of righteousness. . . ." (2 Tim. 4:7–8). How can Paul proclaim victory and say that he is a chief sinner at the same time?

Just a few months before his death, Paul stated that he is (not was) the chief sinner. According to Romans 6, however, Paul did not state that acts of sin were occurring in his life. He simply recognized that flesh within itself has no capability to live. When it perceives that it can live, sin always occurs. With Adam and Eve "coming alive" to their own perceived self, Paul, the descendant of Adam and Eve by his natural birth, was "sold under sin" (Rom. 7:14).

This is not to say that he was under the bondage of sin: "For the law of the Spirit of life in Christ Jesus hath made [him] free from the law of sin and death" (Rom. 8:2). As long as Paul could remain dead to himself, he was "free from sin" (Rom. 6:7). As long as Jesus lived for Paul and not Paul for Jesus, he was righteous (Gal. 3:20–21). "For if we have been planted together in the likeness of his death, we shall be also in the likeness of his resurrection" (Rom. 6:5). Paul, the sinner, could live free from sin because his "old man [the old way of doing things in his own perceived ability was] crucified with [Christ], that the body of sin might be destroyed, that henceforth [he] should not serve sin" (Rom. 6:6).

Challenge. As long as Paul could remain dead (not only to sin, but to himself), he could be free from sin, because Jesus would have the liberty to live within him "that the righteousness of the law might be fulfilled in [Paul], who walk[ed] not after the flesh, but after the Spirit" (Rom. 8:4). If flesh (the attempt to live for God in his own perceived ability) rose up in Paul, however, he knew sin would occur: "For I delight in the law of God after the inward man: But I see another law in my members, warring against the law of my mind, and bringing me into captivity to the law of sin which is in my members" (Rom. 7:22–23).

Because Paul, as with all men, was born a sinner, he knew there was no good in him, that is, in his flesh. He knew the greatest challenge of a Christian was to remain dead to himself. The believer must never experience the "coming alive" to self, even if it is to attempt to live for God. Paul knew the temptation, at first, would not be to do evil, but it would be to do good. It would be a good-versus-good struggle.

In order to have a sin-free life and fulfill the righteousness of the law, every believer must become "crucified with Christ: nevertheless [they will live]; yet not [them], but Christ [living in them]" (Gal. 2:20). The life of every believer must be exchanged for Christ's life. Life is only within Jesus.

Answer. Jesus said, "Verily, verily, I say unto you, He that heareth my word, and believeth on him that sent me, hath everlasting life, and shall not come into condemnation; but is passed from death unto life" (John 5:24). What it means to be Christian is to pass (the original word means "to exchange") from death to life. The old life of the sinner is exchanged for the new life of Christ.

The old man is not made over. He is exchanged! Adam does not attempt to live for Christ. Adam must be crucified with Christ, so that the new man can live. Adam is not raised in resurrection. It is Christ that comes forth from the dead. The old man (Adam) must stay dead, in order that the new man (Christ) can live.

It should be obvious why self-righteousness (the good deeds that believers do for Christ) is so destructive. It is Adam coming alive. It is the struggle of the fall in the Garden of Eden all over again. It is Adam attempting to live. Eternal life, life that continually lives, can be experienced only when He who is life, lives.

Grace lives! "I am crucified with Christ: nevertheless I live; yet not I, but Christ liveth in me . . . I do not frustrate the grace of God. . . ." (Gal. 2:20–21). Jesus said, "Come unto me, all ye that labour [attempting to live in one's own perceived ability] and are heavy laden [frustration, failure, and death], and I will give you rest" (Matt. 11:28).

Amazingly, marvelously, rest from labor does not mean labor stops. It means the believer stops. He rests. Labor continues, but now it is He, who has the capability to do, that is laboring. He who is the essence of all things now takes His rightful place: ". . . seeing he giveth to all life, and breath, and all things. . . . For in him we live, and move, and have our being. . . ." (Acts 17:25, 28).

Jesus Christ living in man, for man is the grace of God. Jesus Christ is the divine provision by which creation is enabled to fulfill its intended purpose. Jesus Christ is life.

Frustration of Grace

Jesus Christ is continual life! John, the disciple that probably had the closest relationship with Jesus during His earthly ministry, knew Jesus as life. This disciple, who wrote more about Jesus than any of His other followers during His earthly walk, began his writings proclaiming the life of Jesus.

> *In the beginning was the Word, and the Word was with God, and the Word was God. The same was in the beginning with God. All things were made by him; and without him was not any thing made that was made. In him was life; and the life was the light of men* (John 1:1–4).

John concluded his writings with the life of Jesus:

> *And the Spirit and the bride say, Come. And let him that heareth say, Come. And let him that is athirst come, And whosoever will, let him take the water of life freely. For I testify unto every man that heareth the words of the prophecy of this book, If any man shall add unto these*

things, God shall add unto him the plagues that are written in this book: And if any man shall take away from the words of the book of this prophecy, God shall take away his part out of the book of life, and out of the holy city, and from the things which are written in this book. He which testifieth these things saith, Surely I come quickly. Amen. Even so, come, Lord Jesus. The grace of our Lord Jesus Christ be with you all. Amen (Rev. 22:17–21).

John not only opened and closed his writings with the life of Jesus; it was also the central theme of John's writing. He closed his gospel with this statement:

And many other signs truly did Jesus in the presence of his disciples, which are not written in this book: But these are written, that ye might believe that Jesus is the Christ, the Son of God; and that believing ye might have life through his name (John 20:30–31).

Probably the most quoted verse in John's writings, perhaps in all of the Bible, speaks of life: "For God so loved the world, that he gave his only begotten Son, that whosoever believeth in him should not perish, but have everlasting life" (John 3:16). Amazingly, John proclaimed that those who believe in Jesus shall not perish ("to destroy fully," translated by KJV as "destroy, die, lose, mar, and perish"), but they have everlasting (perpetual) life. Jesus Christ produces the continual abundant life that does not perish.

Jesus Himself said, ". . . I am come that they might have life, and that they might have it more abundantly" (John 10:10). In turn, Jesus' statement was reflected by Paul in his writings: "For if by one man's offence death reigned by one; much more they which receive abundance of grace and of the gift of righteousness shall reign in life by one, Jesus Christ" (Rom. 5:17).

Regardless of the circumstances, the believer, through Jesus, should reign in life. He should experience the continual life that does not perish when circumstances are bad. The experiencing of life should not rule the believer. The life of Jesus in the believer should reign over the experiences. Paul's own life illustrated this profound truth. He wrote:

> *We are troubled on every side, yet not distressed; we are perplexed, but not in despair; Persecuted, but not forsaken; cast down, but not destroyed . . . For all things are for your sakes, that the abundant grace might . . . redound to the glory of God (2 Cor. 4:8–9, 15).*

Sadly, however, the reality of far too many Christians is not one of continual abundant life but rather one of peaks and valleys. Frustration, stress, and despair surface far too often in the lives of many believers. Many Christians often find themselves reacting to life much the same as the nonbeliever. When circumstances are good, the feelings are on a "high." When circumstances get tough, the joy of the believer falls with the circumstances. Unfortunately, the emotional life of far too many Christians rises and falls with the circumstances they face. Like the unbeliever, the experiences of life often dictate to the believer rather than the believer reigning in life.

Why do so many believers experience so much frustration, stress, and despair when the promise of life is so prevalent? Why do Christians struggle with circumstances when the essence of Christianity is life? How does one get to the place that he can be ". . . troubled on every side, yet not distressed . . . perplexed, but not in despair; Persecuted, but not forsaken; cast down, but not destroyed" (2 Cor. 4:8)?

Insight into this mystery of life is in the often overlooked phrases of "abundance of grace" (Rom. 5:17) and "abundant grace" (2 Cor. 4:15). Additional clues to the mystery can be found in another grace statement of Paul: "I am crucified with Christ: nevertheless I live; yet not I, but Christ liveth in me. . . . I do not frustrate the grace of God. . . ." (Gal. 2:20–21). Finally, Paul said, "But by the grace of God I am what I am: and his grace which was bestowed upon me was not in vain. . . ." (1 Cor. 15:10).

Paul did not "frustrate the grace of God." Consequently, the "abundance of grace" was not bestowed upon him in vain. The free flow of grace in his life enabled him to reign continually over the experiences in life. Trouble, perplexities, pressure, and being cast down did not produce stress, despair, a sense of being forsaken, or destroyed. He experienced the continual abundant life of Jesus Christ by the grace of God.

Struggle of Being Christian

When the Christian comes face to face with the reality of living and successfully conquers the challenge, there is mystery involved: trouble does not produce stress. Circumstances that normally produce death somehow work for a greater life (2 Cor. 4:17). The mystery of grace proclaims that if the believer attempts to live life from within himself (from within the circumstances), the continual life of Jesus perishes. If the believer's "quickening essence" of life is not in the circumstances, however, he experiences the life of Jesus. Continual, abundant life is always dependent upon how one faces his circumstances.

The experiencing of life always seems to set up opposing forces of energy at work in the believer. The struggle to experience life on its basic level is a question of "Who is the source of life?" The Christian, as well as all men, attempts to live life either by the self-life or the Christ-life.

The self-life versus the Christ-life is not exactly two opposing life sources, however. Although the struggle seems to involve two opposing forces, it must be understood that the self-life has no inherent life from within itself. Jesus said, "For as the Father hath life in himself: so hath he given to the Son to have life in himself; And hath given him authority to execute judgment also, because he is the Son of man" (John 5:26–27). Only God has life from within Himself. There is no other source of life.

Man, who has no life within himself, can experience life because the Son of God, who has life within Himself, became the Son of man (life came to man). Without the Son of God, there is no life. Man lives because he has been "set" with the Son of God (Col. 1:17).

The struggle of life occurs because man, once he has experienced the life that is only in Christ, claims that life as if it were his own. The self-life is not a life that lives out of its own power. It is a life of obstinate denial of Christ as the only source of life. The heinousness of sin is when man, who only experiences life because of the Son of God, perceives the life of the Son as his own life.

SELF-LIFE VS. CHRIST-LIFE. Before dealing with the actual struggle of how man perceives himself, it is imperative the believer understands the struggle of being Christian is not one of good versus evil. It is not being trapped in the futile struggle of trying to do good as opposed to doing evil (Rom. 7). The struggle of the mystery of life, the mystery of grace, is one of good versus good. How is the good life produced?

The moral man (one who understands it is best for the good of society, as well as for his own good, to live by some kind of moral code) struggles with a good-versus-evil dilemma. Although good must be done for the welfare of the individual and society, it seems evil always rises to mar the good intentions of the moral man. The mystery of life, the mystery of grace, is not a good-versus-evil issue, however.

Battleground. Christians, in the purest sense of the term, do not struggle with the issue of good versus evil. Although, in reality, many believers readily admit that most of their battles transpire on the level of trying to keep from doing evil, the true warfare of Christianity is fought at a much higher plane. Evil, and the preceding struggle to conquer the temptation to do evil, only occur in the life of the believer after the battle of good versus good has been fought and lost.

Living in holiness. Christians should be holy and should not be struggling with sin. The struggle with sin occurs only after the believer has lost the battle on the plane of holiness. Something has to occur in the life of the believer that moves him out of the realm of Spirit-controlled living, before acts of sin can occur. An act of sin does not cause the believer to fall from holiness; the fall from holiness enables an act of sin to occur.

Losing holiness. Acts of sin cannot occur when the Holy Spirit controls, Christ lives, and grace flows in the believer, producing holiness. Something has to move the believer off the plateau of holiness before an act of sin can happen. It cannot be acts of evil, for evil does not dwell where holiness abounds. Evil occurs only after grace is frustrated, Christ is not allowed to live, and the Holy Spirit is quenched. Therefore, the ultimate conflict of Christianity, the ultimate conflict of life, dwells in the realm of "goodness."

WHO LIVES THE GOOD LIFE? The dilemma that every Christian faces when he is confronted with day-to-day living is "How does he live his life?" Who is the source in overcoming the struggle to experience life? Is good to be accomplished by the perceived ability of the Christian? Is good to be accomplished by that which Christ has done for and in the Christian? Or is good to be accomplished by Christ? Will Jesus Christ be the Way?

This dilemma is the heartbeat of what it means to be Christian. It is the cornerstone of the gospel of Christ. It is coming to grips with the mysteries of life, the mystery of grace.

Self cannot overcome self. The sad reality is that the standard of holiness can never reproduce itself. In fact, the attempt by man to meet the standard by keeping the standard is far more damaging than just the outward manifestation of self-righteousness. The very attempt to be holy, to overcome immorality in one's own ability, actually sows seeds of defeat and assures that continual acts of sin will occur. Man's perceived acts of holiness actually frustrate grace, quench the Spirit, and prohibit Christ from living in him. The Christian moves off the plane of holiness and slides down through self-righteousness into the valley of sin.

Self-righteousness produces acts of sin. An act of sin does not occur where Christ lives, grace flows, and the Spirit controls. Therefore, a long time before an act of sin occurs in the life of the Christian, self slowly begins to take control. The control by self does not manifest itself, at first, in acts of sin but in acts of holiness. The mystery of grace proclaims that acts of sin are not the problem. They are the product of a far greater problem: man attempting to produce life from within his own control.

Conclusion. The true struggle of mankind is "Who lives the life of Christlikeness?" Since self can never overcome self, the self-life must be totally dead. The Christ-life must have freedom to live. The dilemma of the self-life versus the Christ-life, fought on the battleground of whom does good, is indeed the very essence of what it means to be a true believer.

Fighting the battle on the wrong front (good versus evil) always assures the valleys of frustration, stress, and despair. Fighting the battle on the right front (good versus good) at least brings the believer into the arena where victory can be won and continual abundant life can be experienced. The struggle of the dilemma of good versus good is the mystery of life, the mystery of grace.

Lucifer Principle

The dilemma of how one lives the life of Christlikeness is clothed in mystery. Because there is mystery, the drifting from the high plane of holiness is so subtle that a believer, a local church, or an entire denominational structure can be dying and not even know it. Like the freshly cut long-stem rose that appears to be just as beautiful and alive as the roses still on the bush, the unsuspecting can already be separated from the source of life and in the dying process. Even though acts of Christlikeness may be occurring, death has begun because the essence of life, Christ, has been circumvented.

ESSENCE OF THE FALL. Creation experiences life only in its oneness with the Creator, who is the only essence of life. Paul stated that "it pleased the Father that in him [the Son of God] should all fulness dwell" (Col. 1:19). All that exists, exists in and through the Son of God: ". . . all things were created by him and for him: And he is before all things, and by him all things consist [original word means 'to set together']" (Col. 1:16–17). John recorded, "All things were made by him; and without him was not any thing made that was made" (John 1:3). When the events of creation materialized, creation had life because it existed in God. Creation had been "set" with God.

One with God. This is not to say that God became creation and creation became God. A vast chasm exists between the Creator and creation, so that man (the epitome of creation, but nevertheless still creation) cannot comprehend even the chasm, let alone the mystery that spans the chasm. Even though the mystery of oneness spans the great gulf, creation is always creation and the Creator is always the Creator. Moreover, the distinctiveness of the Creator and creation must always be maintained, for to do otherwise is idolatry. (See Exod. 20:3–5.)

It is to say that, although the distinct Creator and that which God produced as distinct creation are two separate entities, they exist in so much oneness that the life that is in the Creator is experienced in the creation. The revelation of the essence of this oneness is the key that unlocks the mystery of life, the mystery of grace, and all things that exist. Life is only in oneness with God because God is the only One that is life.

The awakening of man. Just as the freshly cut rose only appears to have life, the reality of death for man is also already occurring when there is a separation from the life source. This deadly truth has as its foundation the "awakening" of creation to itself. It is the "big lie," the faulty concept that life itself can exist in creation.

When man (through his God-given freedom to reject God) began to think his life was not in his oneness with the Creator, but rather in himself, he began to "awake to himself." At some point in the experiencing of life, man began to perceive that he could assume control of that life. Man began to glory in the life he was experiencing as if it was his life. Failing to give glory to the Source of life, man lived as if he was the source. He began to take "the name of the Lord [his] God in vain . . ." (Exod. 20:7). He began to die.

Becoming as gods. Instead of keeping his distinctiveness in the equation of oneness with God, he attempted to become as God. For example, before the fall, he had eyes that were blind, yet he saw (experienced life). When his eyes were opened (awakened), he became blind (experienced death). Thus, Jesus said, ". . . For judgment I am come into this world, that they which see not might see; and that they which see might be made blind. And some of the Pharisees which were with him heard these words, and said unto him, Are we blind also? Jesus said unto them, If ye were blind, ye should have no sin: but now ye say, We see; therefore your sin remaineth" (John 9:39–41).

The awakening of man to his own identity as a perceived self drove a wedge into the oneness of the mystery of life. In "seeing," he separated himself from the essence of life, the One who sees. Man's quest for life in himself actually brought death to himself. He succumbed to the same truth that brought Lucifer down. (See Ezek. 28; Isa. 14.)

EVIL PRINCIPLE. The essence of becoming blind by attempting to see (dying by attempting to live—even in what God had done) is the epitome of evil. Evil always occurs when the process of life is attempted by man to be "turned over": "Among whom also we all had our conversation [translated from a word meaning 'to overturn'] in times past in the lusts of our flesh, fulfilling the desires of the flesh and of the mind. . . ." (Eph. 2:3). Man's attempt to live by his own seeing produced the opposite results. It produced evil, an "overturn." The English language catches the significance: *l–i–v–e* "overturned" is *e–v–i–l*.

Moreover, the personification of this overturn is the devil. He who once lived in ultimate existence ("Thou sealest up the sum, full of wisdom, and perfect in beauty" [Ezek. 28:12]) became the degradation of hell (Isa. 14:15). He became the "overturn," the devil. The English, again, catches the significance: *l–i–v–e–d* "overturned" is the *d–e–v–i–l*. The attempted ascent of the creature to live as the Creator always brings life down to the lowest hell (Isa. 14:15). It is idolatry of the highest order.

This same principle can be seen in the devil's temptation of Jesus:

And the devil, taking him up into an high mountain, shewed unto him all the kingdoms of the world in a moment of time. And the devil said unto him, All this power will I give thee, and the glory of them: for that is delivered unto me; and to whomsoever I will I give it. If thou therefore wilt worship me, all shall be thine (Luke 4:5–7).

The power, the glory, and the kingdom that belong only to the Creator must never be sought by the creature. This thirst for power and glory to be experienced within the creature itself, first manifested by Lucifer, always produces the fall.

This Lucifer Principle is not some vague philosophical fantasy. Sadly, it is the reality of the struggle of the creature. Without a doubt, it is the reason why far too many Christians stumble, far too many local churches stagnate, and denominations continue to deteriorate. It is the reality of every fall.

Temptation. The Lucifer Principle is also illustrated when Jesus gave a rather surprising answer to a joyful statement by His disciples. When the disciples "returned . . . with joy, saying, Lord, even the devils are subject unto us through thy name," Jesus responded, ". . . I beheld Satan as lightning falling from heaven." He continued, "Behold, I give you power . . . over all the power of the enemy. . . . Notwithstanding in this rejoice not, that the spirits are subject unto you; but rather rejoice, because your names are written in heaven" (Luke 10:17–20).

Why does Jesus respond this way? Could it be that He recognized the beginning of the Lucifer Principle being manifested in the lives of the disciples? The disciples were excited over devils being subject to them. They were actually experiencing the joy of life in Jesus Christ. They were experiencing the result of oneness with the essence of life, the Son of God. Why, then, did Jesus respond as he did?

Victim of the blessing. Jesus' response pinpointed the danger for all creation. The life in the Creator is so powerful that it transforms everything. Creation, which had no life, now gloriously experiences life. It was nothing, but now it experiences everything. When creation experiences the "everything" of God, the "everything" is so potent it leaves the creature susceptible to a powerful temptation.

Creation becomes tempted to perceive that it has something to do with the life it now enjoys. It actually begins to try to live in what God has done for it. What God had done was to produce creation, a new creation, the only creation. Being able to experience the life of the created work of God, the creature begins to perceive that he can live in the life he is experiencing itself. Forgetting the Source of life, the creature becomes a victim of his own blessing. The creature's quest for life in himself actually brings death to himself. Consequently the fall occurs.

Answer. The Lucifer Principle is subtle. Jesus said, "Behold, I give unto you power to tread on serpents and scorpions, and over all the power of the enemy: and nothing shall by any means hurt you" (Luke 10:19). He also said, however, "Notwithstanding in this [devils being subject to the believers and all that is involved in that subjection] rejoice not . . . but rather rejoice, because your names are written in heaven" (Luke 10:20).

Nothing can hurt the believer because he is one with the One who has had all things already put under His feet by the Father (Eph. 1:22). The believer has authority over devils and should live in that authority; however, it is not his authority, but the Authority that resides in him. The believer is one with Jesus. He lives because Jesus lives.

Believers must live in the life that is in the Creator and not awaken to a perceived life in the self, a perceived life in what God has done within him. The awakening of self is the beginning of all that is death and dying. Christians, and the church as a whole, in their zeal to live the victorious life over devils and demons, must not fail to perceive that life is only in the Creator. Jesus, and Jesus alone, has life. To believe anything else is to fall into the deathtrap of the Lucifer Principle.

Frustration of Grace

The apostle Paul characterized this struggle within man in his letter to the Galatians:

> *I am crucified with Christ {self-life dead}: nevertheless I live; yet not I, but Christ liveth in me: and the life which I now live in the flesh I live by the faith of the Son of God, who loved me, and gave himself for me. I do not frustrate the grace of God: for if righteousness come by the law {Christlikeness attempted in man's own perceived capability}, then Christ is dead in vain* (Gal. 2:20–21).

This issue of not frustrating the grace of God, evolving out of the Lucifer Principle, was such an important issue in the first century church that the entire letter of Galatians was written to warn of its consequences.

GRACE VS. FLESH. After Paul gave his personal testimony in the Galatians letter, he entered into the primary reason for writing it. He stated, "Knowing that a man is not justified by the works of the law, but by the faith of Jesus Christ, even we have believed in Jesus Christ, that we might be justified by the faith of Christ, and not by the works of the law . . ." (Gal. 2:16).

A key phrase in understanding this letter and understanding frustrated grace is "works of the law." The same emphasis is given when Paul stated, "I do not frustrate the grace of God: for if righteousness come by the law, then Christ is dead in vain" (2: 21). To understand the phrases "works of the law" and "if righteousness come by the law, then Christ is dead in vain" is to understand the essence of Paul's letter to the Galatians. It is also the understanding of that which frustrates grace. It is the beginning of the understanding of the mysteries of grace.

Grace of God. Near the beginning of the Galatian letter, Paul asked a rather penetrating question: "This only would I learn of you, Received ye the Spirit by the works of the law, or by the hearing of faith?" (Gal. 3:2). Paul asked the saints, "I just want to know one thing. How did you get saved? How did the Spirit of Christ come into your life? Was it by works (self-righteousness), or was it through the hearing of faith, the gospel message?"

The response to that question came easily. Paul had previously stated, "I marvel that ye are so soon removed from him that called you into the grace of Christ. . . ." (Gal. 1:6). Moreover, the essence of Paul's message to the Galatians was no doubt the same gospel he wrote about to the Ephesians: "For by grace are ye saved through faith; and that not of yourselves: it is the gift of God: Not of works, lest any man should boast" (Eph. 2:8–9).

Paul told the Ephesians they were not saved by works. They were saved by grace through faith. Since Paul did not answer his initial question to the Galatians, he assumed they would know how they became Christians. They also were saved by grace through faith.

Paul's next question to the Galatians is the key to understanding "frustrated grace." He wrote, "Are ye so foolish? having begun in the Spirit, are ye now made perfect by the flesh?" (Gal. 3:3). The word *perfect* is the standard word used in the New Testament for Christian maturity. It literally means arriving at the end of that for which you were intended or being made complete. It simply means becoming all you can become in Jesus Christ. One who is perfect is a mature Christian.

Paul asked the Galatian saints, "How does a believer become a perfected saint?" Another way to ask this series of questions is "How did you get saved; how do you stay saved?" Paul probed for an understanding of the very heart of what it means to be Christian. He was exploring the mysteries of grace.

Flesh of man. How does one become a mature Christian? Does a Christian develop into spiritual maturity "by the flesh" (Gal. 3:3)? What does the phrase "by the flesh" mean? Paul later explained, "For it is written, that Abraham had two sons, the one by a bondmaid, the other by a freewoman. But he who was of the bondwoman was born after the flesh. . . ." (Gal: 4:22–23). Abraham did not go into Hagar because he could not control his biological glands. Dirty, rotten desires (a common misunderstanding of the meaning of flesh) were not the motivation for a son being born of the bondwoman.

God had promised a child to Abraham and Sarah in their old age. The son, however, did not come immediately after the promise was given. So what did Abraham and Sarah do? They decided to "help God out" in His promise to give them a child.

Abraham and Sarah erred in attempting to help God in the fulfilling of the promise. Abraham going into Hagar was the product of the error. Just look at the pain, agony, and death that perceived-to-be-noble act of helping God out has caused the world. The flesh always brings frustration, stress, and despair.

Abraham and Sarah's attempt to help God out in the fulfilling of His promise is a vital clue in understanding the flesh. Additional insight can also come from Paul's final admonition to the Galatians: "Stand fast therefore in the liberty wherewith Christ hath made us free, and be not entangled again with the yoke of bondage" (Gal. 5:1). What is this "yoke of bondage"?

After encouraging the Galatians to "be not entangled again with the yoke of bondage," Paul wrote:

Behold, I Paul say unto you, that if ye be circumcised, Christ shall profit you nothing. For I testify again to every man that is circumcised, that he is a debtor to do the whole law. Christ is become of no effect unto you, whosoever of you are justified by the law; ye are fallen from grace (Gal. 5:2–4).

It should be obvious that the "yoke of bondage" and "fallen from grace" are correlated. In fact, falling from grace is inseparably tied to the yoke of bondage.

What a tremendous shame to be a Christian and have Christ profit the believer nothing (Gal. 5:2). How pitiful to have Christ and have Him become of no effect (5: 4). When man attempts to live in his own ability (the flesh), grace is frustrated and bondage is experienced.

This is the reason Jesus said, "Come unto me, all ye that labour and are heavy laden, and I will give you rest. Take my yoke upon you. . . ." (Matt. 11:28–29). The flesh can never produce spiritual maturity, for it is the attempt to live in one's own yoke. The flesh always produces bondage ("heavy laden"-ness). Living in the yoke of Jesus as opposed to the believer's yoke is what it means to be Christian. It is understanding the mysteries of grace.

Liberty or bondage? Paul admonished the Galatians: "Stand fast therefore in the liberty wherewith Christ hath made us free, and be not entangled again with the yoke of bondage" (Gal. 5:1). What is this liberty? It is not a liberty "to do as one pleases." It is a liberty from the law of sin and death, a liberty from the moral imperfections that keep the believer from reigning in life. It is a liberty from the problems of struggling Christians, a liberty from bondage.

Paul said to the Galatians: "If we live in the Spirit, let us also walk in the Spirit" (Gal. 5:25). The believer must "not be weary in well doing . . ." (Gal. 6:9) and must "fulfil the law of Christ" (Gal. 6:2). The liberty the believer experiences is not unlicensed freedom. It is a liberty, for the first time in the believer's life, in which the believer through Jesus Christ can do as he ought.

Unfortunately, most Christians unknowingly frustrate grace by attempting to produce righteousness in their own ability. They frustrate life by attempting to live life themselves. Paul stated that believers must "through the Spirit wait for the hope of righteousness by faith" (Gal. 5:5). Grace, when it is not frustrated produces the continual abundant life of righteousness that eliminates the "roller-coaster" life of frustration, stress, and despair. Christ can be effective and profitable in the life of every believer when grace is not frustrated.

A STRUGGLE. Paul continued to emphasize the free flow of grace in the remaining verses of Galatians 5. The essence of the struggle is stated here: "For the flesh lusteth against the Spirit, and the Spirit against the flesh: and these are contrary the one to the other: so that ye cannot do the things that ye would" (Gal. 17).

Without question, there is a struggle in the Christian walk. Unfortunately, most Christians confront the struggle on the wrong front. Many Christians interpret Christianity as being the struggle to put down the flesh (interpreted as "bad things") and lift up the Spirit (interpreted as "good things"). The struggle for these misguided Christians is a struggle of good versus evil. Their entire life seems to be spent in fighting to do good and not bad. Sadly, every time the Christian fights the battle on that plane, evil eventually wins. Not doing the things that should be done and doing the things that should not be done is a telltale sign that grace has already been frustrated.

Spirit or flesh? Paul gave a vital point in understanding Christianity when he wrote, "This I say then, Walk in the Spirit, and ye shall not fulfil the lust of the flesh" (Gal. 5:16). The lust of the flesh is not conquered by struggling with the flesh. Flesh can never overcome the flesh. It is only defeated by the "walk in the Spirit." The walk in the Spirit is the Spirit producing the fruit of righteousness in the believer. It is letting Christ live in the believer for the believer.

The phrase "the lust of the flesh" means that the self has a strong, passionate desire to live for itself in its own ability or to live for God in its own ability. In Galatians 4 (concerning Abraham, Sarah, and Hagar), Paul indicated that flesh meant, "helping God out" by doing what is right, simply because it needs to be done. Paul also indicated this same truth: "I do not frustrate the grace of God: for if righteousness come by the law, then Christ is dead in vain" (Gal. 2:21). If man could live by the law in his own ability, then there would have been no need for Christ to have come into this world to give His life.

Man cannot live right in his own ability, however. It was necessary for Christ to die upon the cross in order that man's sins could be forgiven and he could be declared righteous. It was also necessary for Christ to be raised from the dead to live within man, thereby enabling man to experience righteous living. This is what it means to be Christian: Christ died for man's sins; Christ lives for man's righteousness.

Paul illustrated this great struggle between spirit and flesh by carrying the contrast to its conclusion. He wrote, "Now the works of the flesh are manifest, which are these: Adultery, fornication, uncleanness, lasciviousness . . . and such like . . ." (Gal. 5:19–21). Many have understood the "works of the flesh" as adultery, fornication, uncleanness, and the rest of the list in verses 19-21. Adultery, fornication, uncleanness, etc. are the manifestations that occur when a believer attempts to live for God in his own ability (works of the flesh).

Paul compared the Spirit's work (fruit, Gal. 5:22) with the flesh's work (manifest, Gal. 5: 19), just as he has already compared liberty with bondage and Spirit with flesh. The work of the Spirit produces life (love, joy, peace, longsuffering, gentleness, goodness, faith, meekness, temperance); and the works of the flesh produce death (adultery, fornication, uncleanness, lasciviousness, etc.). When grace flows, the believer experiences the fruit of the Spirit. When grace is frustrated by the works of the flesh (living for God in his own ability), the believer experiences the list in verses 19–21.

Obviously, these manifestations of sin are not the problem. They are the product of the problem. The real problem is the frustration of grace by the works of the flesh.

Failure mechanism. The phrase "so that ye cannot do the things that ye would" is a reality in the lives of far too many Christians because grace is frustrated. Mysteriously, the attempt to do what needs to be done, and man's zeal to help God out in the living of life, actually frustrate grace. Grace is frustrated out of man's own attempted goodness, the works of the flesh.

Attempting to help God out has a built-in failure mechanism. Since a life of holiness is a production of the grace of God, grace that is frustrated cannot produce holiness. Since the Christ-life is quenched by the self-life, life is always experienced in what the self is, a sinner. Sin always occurs when self is in control, even if the control is geared toward God. Although the intentions are good, the end result of man's effort is always the valley of frustration, stress, and despair.

Answer. Understanding this great truth is paramount for understanding what it means to be Christian. Every believer who struggles with stress, despair, a feeling of being forsaken, or a sense of perishing from the circumstances of life experiences frustrated grace. Christ, who dwells within the believer, is not having the freedom to be effective and profitable to produce the continual abundant life.

The cure for the valley of frustration, stress, and despair is having the free flow of grace. The believer must experience a deeper realm of oneness with Christ. He must experience the reality of the exchanged life, the believer's yoke exchanged for the yoke of Christ. He must understand that all of his own efforts (even though they may be done with the best of intentions) must cease. He must come to understand Jesus Christ as the Way.

There is only one pathway to experiencing all the blessings of God, the reality of reigning in life. Paul gave it when he wrote:

> *I am crucified with Christ: nevertheless I live; yet not I, but Christ liveth in me: and the life which I now live in the flesh I live by the faith of the Son of God, who loved me, and gave himself for me. I do not frustrate the grace of God . . .* (Gal. 2:20–21).

Paul simply stated that he did not attempt to live for Christ. Paul experienced life; however, he lived because Christ lived in him.

Paul was "crucified with Christ," meaning the transformation process did not change him, improve him, or make him over. It completely did away with him. He was dead in Christ, yet he experienced life because he was one with the resurrected Christ who lives. Moreover, it was not even based upon the faith of Paul, but, in fact, it was "by the faith of the Son of God." Finally, Paul lived because he did not frustrate grace. Christ did not die in vain. Christ was effective. Christ was profitable.

What a powerful message of good news! Jesus Christ is the Way. He has done it all. Every believer can "stand fast in the liberty wherewith Christ hath made [them] free." They are free to live, free to experience the continual abundant life in Jesus Christ! They are free from the bondage of frustration, stress, and despair simply because the grace of God has not been frustrated. They are free in Jesus Christ, the Way.

chapter 4

Revelation of Grace

Why do two people sitting under the same message respond to it so differently? Does God withhold His revelation from one while allowing another to receive it?

Why does a particular passage of Scripture suddenly "leap off the page" and speak powerful revelation to one's heart, although it has been read many times before? Does God delight in causing us to search continually while doling out nuggets of truth only in bits and pieces?

Why does it seem so difficult to learn the ways of God? Does God have respect of persons? If not, why then does it seem one person knows more or learns faster than another?

Paradox of Christian Learning

In experiencing the revelation of God, an amazing paradox is largely unknown by most Christians. Jesus indicated this mystery of experiencing God when He said:

. . . I thank thee, O Father, Lord of heaven and earth, that thou hast hid these things from the wise and prudent, and hast revealed them unto babes: even so, Father; for so it seemed good in thy sight. . . . And he turned him unto his disciples, and said privately, Blessed are the eyes which see the things that ye see: For I tell you, that many prophets and kings have desired to see those things which ye see, and have not seen them; and to hear those things which ye hear, and have not heard them (Luke 10:21, 23–24).

There is something definitely mysterious in the eyes of the prophets and the kings of Israel that saw not and in their ears that heard not.

They perceived themselves to be as a nation, the one true seeker of God. Paul wrote:

Behold, thou art called a Jew, and restest in the law, and makest thy boast of God, and knowest his will, and approvest the things that are more excellent, being instructed out of the law; And art confident that thou thyself art a guide of the blind, a light of them which are in darkness (Rom. 2:17–19).

How they saw themselves was not how God saw them, however. ". . . All day long I have stretched forth my hands unto a disobedient and gainsaying people" (Rom. 10:21). They were hearing, but they were hearing amiss and even obstinate in their faulty hearing. In fact, Paul added, ". . . Israel hath not obtained that which he seeketh for. . . ." (Rom. 11:7). They actively sought God, but somehow in their seeking they did not find Him. They misunderstood the unique, godly principle that receiving the revelation of God is by the grace of God.

SEARCHING FOR GOD. The question has been raised, "Canst thou by searching find out God? canst thou find out the Almighty unto perfection?" (Job 11:7). Paul raised the same query: "Where is the wise? where is the scribe? where is the disputer of this world? hath not God made foolish the wisdom of this world? For after that in the wisdom of God the world by wisdom knew not God. . . ." (1 Cor. 1:20–21).

One of the foundational truths of the ways of God is that the wisdom of this world is not capable of "finding out God." Regardless of how hard the mind may seek, the wisdom of man cannot cross the great chasm into the mind of God. In fact, Paul recorded this statement of God to Moses, ". . . I will have mercy on whom I will have mercy, and I will have compassion on whom I will have compassion. So then it is not of him that willeth, nor of him that runneth, but of God that sheweth mercy" (Rom. 9:15–16). The secret in finding God lies not in the determination and effort of man but rests in the mercy of God.

Self-disclosure of God. If man cannot find out God by his own seeking and searching, then any knowledge of God that is acquired by man has to come from God's own revelation of Himself. If God had never chosen to reveal Himself, man could never come to know God or anything concerning Him. Paul wrote:

> *But as it is written, Eye hath not seen, nor ear heard, neither have entered into the heart of man, the things which God hath prepared for them that love him. But God hath revealed them unto us by his Spirit: for the Spirit searcheth all things, yea, the deep things of God. For what man knoweth the things of a man, save the spirit of man which is in him? even so the things of God knoweth no man, but the Spirit of God. Now we have received, not the spirit of the world, but the spirit which is of God; that we might know the things that are freely given to us of God. Which things also we speak, not in the words which man's wisdom teacheth, but which the Holy Ghost teacheth; comparing spiritual things with spiritual. But the natural man receiveth not the things of the Spirit of God: for they are foolishness unto him: neither can he know them, because they are spiritually discerned. But he that is spiritual judgeth all things, yet he himself is judged of no man. For who*

hath known the mind of the Lord, that he may instruct him? But we have the mind of Christ (1 Cor. 2:9–16).

For man to acquire any knowledge of God, God has to be the giver of that knowledge.

In other words, man learns of God as he encounters God through the disclosure of God. God has revealed Himself in a self-opening out of His being. This is the statement of John when he wrote:

And we know that the Son of God is come, and hath given us an under-standing, that we may know him that is true, and we are in him that is true, even in his Son Jesus Christ. This is the true God, and eternal life (1 John 5:20).

If it had not been for the coming of Jesus Christ, the ultimate revelation of God, mankind could never have come to "know him that is true . . . the true God." Although man cannot find out God by his own searching, he can know God because God chose to reveal Himself by His grace.

Drawing back the veil. Again, in his letter to the Corinthians, Paul gave more of his insights into the uniqueness of Christian learning. Speaking concerning the "hidden wisdom" of God (1 Cor. 2:7), Paul wrote, ". . . God hath revealed [it] unto us by his Spirit . . ." (1 Cor. 2:10). The word revealed literally means "a drawing back of the veil." That which had been concealed from man by a veil and could not be penetrated by man's wisdom is now revealed or made known by the drawing back of the veil.

The belief in the existence of God and His revelation are the result of God's initiative. Man could never know of God's existence and experience His revelation if God had not chosen to reveal Himself. Moreover, man receives that revelation of God as he encounters or experiences God. All that man has or knows of God is a result of his experience with God.

Mystery of revelation. Paul recorded another dynamic statement concerning the uniqueness of Christian learning. He recorded a statement of Isaiah who was quoting God, ". . . I was found of them that sought me not; I was made manifest unto them that asked not after me" (Rom. 10:20). This seemingly difficult statement lies at the very heart of understanding the unique Christian approach to God.

Although God stated He was found of them that sought Him not, Jesus said:

> *Ask, and it shall be given you; seek, and ye shall find; knock, and it shall be opened unto you: for everyone that asketh receiveth; and he that seeketh findeth; and to him that knocketh it shall be opened* (Matt. 7:7–8).

These two seemingly contradictory statements (God is found by those who did not seek Him, and Jesus' admonition to seek and it shall be found) can be understood by recognizing that obviously there is a way to seek God that is not "seeking" Him.

FAILURE TO FIND GOD. Moreover, Paul seems to indicate that man's effort to seek God by his own study, skills, or acts of wisdom may actually hinder the process of finding God. He wrote, "For Christ sent me not to baptize, but to preach the gospel: not with wisdom of words, lest the cross of Christ should be made of none effect" (1 Cor. 1:17). His own preaching was ". . . not with enticing words of man's wisdom . . . that . . . faith should not stand in the wisdom of men, but in the power of God" (1 Cor. 2:4–5). Man trying to experience the revelation of God is actually hindered by his attempt to know God through his own skill, will, or determination.

A misunderstanding. Perhaps it would help to clear up a misunderstanding of the most often quoted verse concerning study in the Bible. Paul stated, "Study to shew thyself approved unto God, a workman that needeth not to be ashamed, rightly dividing the word of truth" (2 Tim. 2:15).

Many Christians understand this verse as a command or an admonition of Paul to Timothy to study the Word of God. If the mind of man cannot comprehend the things of God, however, why would Paul encourage Timothy to attempt something that is impossible?

Any good English dictionary will help us understand what Paul really said. All comprehensive English dictionaries give two shades of meaning for the word study. The first one is the more common understanding, "the use of the mind to gain knowledge or the act or process of learning about something" (*Webster's Third New International Dictionary*). The second definition is "to apply the attention and mind to a subject." This second definition comes closer to the meaning of the original language of the New Testament.

"Study to shew." Paul told Timothy to apply his attention, his mind, to the subject of being a workman approved unto God. He did not tell him "to study." More specifically, Paul told Timothy not only to apply his attention, but to make haste about it, for in the original language, the word translated study (actually the phrase "study to shew" is the translation of the original word) means "to make haste, to exert one's self, endeavor, give diligence" (*Webster's Third New International Dictionary*). One is to "study to shew" himself approved. He is to make haste about it.

The entire verse illustrates the meaning. The word approved in this context means a workman who has been put to the test and, meeting the specifications, has won the approval of the one who has subjected him to the test. Thus, Paul actually told Timothy, "Make haste, be approved of God."

Conclusion. A workman such as this, one who is approved, has no cause for shame when he is inspected. The reason he does not need to be ashamed is that he has "rightly handled" (2 Tim. 2:15 NIV) the Word of truth. Rightly handling the Word of truth will produce a workman who is approved by God, because the Word of truth is Jesus. When Jesus is rightly handled, approval is always given. A believer will not be ashamed of himself or of the work, for he will have the approval of God through Jesus Christ.

Finally, there is the urging on, the exhortation to make haste. Thus, the "study to shew" of this verse does not relate to the idea of the use of the mind to gain knowledge. Rather, it is an admonition to hurry up and let God do His work.

Sadly, because many do not understand the process of Christian learning, they actually work against themselves in their study of God's written Word. Man must "get into the Word" and come to understand the ways of God; however, he must realize that understanding the written revelation of God only occurs by divine revelation of Jesus Christ. It will not come by human ingenuity. Man must rightly handle the Word of truth.

Rightly Handling the Word

Perhaps the question of all ages is: "How does one rightly handle the Word?" The answer to that question is given in the form of a parable. Jesus said:

> . . . *Behold, a sower went forth to sow; And when he sowed, some seeds fell by the way side, and the fowls came and devoured them up: Some fell upon stony places, where they had not much earth: and forthwith they sprung up, because they had no deepness of earth: And when the sun was up, they were scorched; and because they had no root, they withered away. And some fell among thorns; and the thorns sprung up, and choked them: But other fell into good ground, and brought forth fruit, some an hundredfold, some sixtyfold, some thirtyfold. Who hath ears to hear, let him hear* (Matt. 13:3–9).

Several verses later, when Jesus explained the parable, He stated:
(1) "when any one heareth the word . . .",
(2) "the same is he that heareth the word . . .",
(3) "he that heareth the word . . .", and again,

(4) "he that heareth the word. . . ." The same sower sows the same kind of seed in all four plantings (Matt. 13:19–20, 22–23).

RESPONDING TO THE WORD. Four different responses occurred, however. The variable in the parable is the condition of the soil, or how one handles the Word. The response to the seed changed as the condition of the soil changed from impenetrable, stony, thorn-infested, and finally, good ground. It is not a coincidence that Jesus closed the parable with the statement, "Who hath ears to hear, let him hear." The various responses seem to be inseparably tied to the condition of the soil in which the seed is sown. The responses are inseparably tied to how one "handles the Word."

The implication is that all have ears to hear, but the hearing of some seems to be impaired. Something restrains the seed from sufficiently penetrating the soil. All responders had ears to hear, but they heard in various degrees.

Jesus further explained:

Hear ye therefore the parable of the sower. When any one heareth the word of the kingdom, and understandeth it not, then cometh the wicked one, and catcheth away that which was sown in his heart. This is he which received seed by the way side. But he that received the seed into stony places, the same is he that heareth the word, and anon with joy receiveth it; Yet hath he not root in himself, but dureth for while: for when tribulation or persecution ariseth because of the word, by and by he is offended. He also that received seed among the thorns is he that heareth the word; and the care of this world, and the deceitfulness of riches, choke the word, and he becometh unfruitful. But he that received seed into the good ground is he that heareth the word, and understandeth it; which also beareth fruit, and bringeth forth, some an hundredfold, some sixty, some thirty (Matt. 13:18–23).

In the first response, one hears the "word of the kingdom, and understandeth it not . . ." Notice that the "wicked one . . . catcheth away that which was sown . . ." only because the seed "fell by the way side."

Because the seed fell on the road and did not penetrate the soil, "the fowls came and devoured them up." The wicked one can seize the seed only if it does not penetrate the heart. If the seed penetrates the heart, or is understood, the wicked one is of no consequence.

Obviously, then, understanding the Word of the kingdom is vitally important. If the Word is understood, it is not stolen away. It bears fruit. Or, as Jesus stated in the fourth response, "But he that received seed into the good ground is he that heareth the word, and understandeth it; which also beareth fruit, and bringeth forth, some an hundredfold, some sixty, some thirty" (v. 23).

Understanding the Word. Understanding the word of the kingdom is vitally important. Moreover, to the degree one fails to understand the Word when it is encountered, is the degree of unfruitfulness of the Word in his life. Understanding the Word is not as it might seem to the mind, however. If the normal meaning for understanding is used, then the prize would go only to the intellectual. The sharper the mind, the greater the reward. Jesus emphatically stated the opposite, however. ". . . I thank thee, O Father, Lord of heaven and earth, that thou hast hid these things from the wise and prudent [learned], and hast revealed them unto babes. . . ." (Luke 10:21).

The word *understandeth,* as found in verses 13:19 (first response) and 13:23 (fourth response), is not the normal word that we might assume as meaning "to understand." Probably most assume that *understandeth* relates to the idea of "to know," "to see," "to put the mind upon," or "to exercise the mind" (all definitions of Greek words translated *understand* by the King James Version). The word *understandeth* in the explanation of Jesus' parable means "to put together." Understanding is obtained because two things come together: the seed (the Word) and the soil (the heart).

Being set with the Word. It is not stretching the point to emphasize that *understandeth,* as Jesus used it in His parable, does not come from an "exercise (of) the mind." Nor does it come from putting "the mind upon" (studying). Neither does it come from knowing by observation. Nor does it come from knowing from knowledge itself. Rather, Christian understanding comes from putting together the Word and the heart. It is the encounter with Truth Himself (an encounter with a Person) that brings understanding.

The power of Christian learning does not come from the exercise or activity of the mind. It comes from the Word itself. The fruit that comes forth from the "putting together" of the seed (Word) and the soil (heart) is from the germinated seed. The fruit does not come forth because the soil has been impregnated. The fruit does not come from the soil. All that is needed to produce the fruit is contained within the seed itself. The fruit comes forth because the seed has been allowed to germinate.

This does not mean that man's mind goes into neutral and never thinks. Jesus' statement does imply, however, that the mind is not the source of man's knowing. Christian learning does not come from knowing by observation or from putting the mind upon (studying). It comes forth because the Word has been allowed to germinate.

A useless mind. Indeed, in the Garden of Eden, it was man's thirst to know by his observation that led to his not knowing. The original word translated *knowledge*, as in the tree of the knowledge of good and evil, gives a vital clue to the deadly disease that kills and impairs hearing. *Knowledge* is translated from a primary word meaning "to know (properly, to ascertain by seeing)." Man desired to know based upon his own observation (his own seeing).

Amazingly, when the use of the mind becomes the basis of understanding, the mind becomes useless in understanding. Before the fall, our parents understood with eyes that did not see. After the fall, they could not understand with eyes that saw. Their eyes had "opened," and they could no longer see.

Jesus addressed this same issue when He said:

> . . . *For judgment I am come into this world, that they which see not might see; and that they which see might be made blind. And some of*

the Pharisees which were with him heard these words, and said unto him, Are we blind also? Jesus said unto them, If ye were blind, ye should have no sin: but now ye say, We see; therefore your sin remaineth (John 9:39–41).

True "seeing" (knowing) is the issue, and how one attempts to experience that seeing is the heart of the issue. Paradoxically, the Christian truly "sees" when he becomes blind. He becomes blind when he attempts to see.

THE BIG LIE. The fall of mankind occurred when Adam and Eve desired to become "as gods" and be their own source of seeing. Scripture records that the serpent:

> *. . . said he unto the woman, Yea, hath God said, Ye shall not eat of every tree of the garden? And the woman said unto the serpent, We may eat of the fruit of the trees of the garden: But of the fruit of the tree which is in the midst of the garden, God hath said, Ye shall not eat of it, neither shall ye touch it, lest ye die. And the serpent {from a primary word that actually implies "whisper a (magic) spell, to prognosticate"} said unto the woman, Ye shall not surely die: For God doth know that in the day ye eat thereof, then your eyes shall be opened, and ye shall be as gods, knowing good and evil. And when the woman saw {something that the human being could only do because the Spirit brought life and light to the "seeing network"} that the tree was good for food, and that it was pleasant {translated from a word meaning "a longing to wish for"} to the eyes, and a tree to be desired {translated from a word meaning "to delight in"} to make one wise {translated from a word meaning "to be circumspect (intelligent)"}, she took of the fruit thereof, and did eat, and gave also unto her husband with her; and he did eat. And the eyes of them both were opened, and they {saw}. . . .* (Gen. 3:1–7).

God had said, "But of the tree of the knowledge of good and evil, thou shalt not eat of it: for in the day that thou eatest thereof thou shalt surely die" (Gen. 2:17). They ate. They saw. They died. The process of dying (likewise, the process of impaired hearing) always occurs when man attempts "to see" based upon his own observations. Jesus said to the Pharisees, ". . . now ye say, We see; therefore your sin remaineth."

Deadly self-perception. When the seed from the sower fell upon the wayside, the condition of the soil would not let it penetrate to germinate. The once receptive soil had been much traveled (*way side* is translated from a word meaning "road"). It had become hardened and impenetrable.

Likewise, a once receptive heart that has been much traveled by the self-seeing of man's mind will become impenetrable. The many offenses of the "fruit that kills" (attempting to live in the fruit of the tree of the knowledge of good and evil) hardens the heart. The once tender heart of the "child" (see Matt. 18:2–14) becomes impenetrable to the Word.

The deadly hiss of self-actualization has brought about the dominance of a life-style that desires to know, not only good and evil, but to assert itself on that perceived knowledge. The self-assertiveness to actualize one's being from self-perception is the deadly disease that kills. The simple message of life in Christ will not be heard by the heart that is caught in the trap of self-actualization. Self-assertiveness will not let the Word penetrate the heart to germinate to everlasting life.

Selfishly handling the Word. Moreover, the parable of the sower seems to indicate that to the degree self-assertiveness manifests itself is the degree to which hearing is impaired. Jesus further explained, "But he that received the seed into stony places, the same is he that heareth the word, and anon with joy receiveth it" (Matt. 13:20). In the second planting, the responder heard the word and at once (anon) received it with joy.

Yet there is still a problem. The parable moved from the man who heard but did not hear (the seed did not penetrate the ground), to the man who heard but his hearing was shallow. He heard (the seed penetrated the soil), but his hearing had no depth of understanding: "And when the sun was up, they were scorched; and because they had no root, they withered away" (Matt. 13:6).

Jesus stated, "Yet hath he not root in himself, but dureth for a while. . . ." (Matt. 13:21). The failure occurred because of the ineptitude of the hearer to let the seed take root. Moreover, because the seed was not allowed to take root, and the hearer himself had no "root in himself," he "dureth for a while." The life he experienced was short lived.

The phrase "dureth for a while" actually is translated from the verb "I exist." The failure of the second responder is correlated to his existence. Because of the hearer's own effort in life, the seed was not able to take root. Consequently, without a root system of the seed, there is an inadequate root system in the self-existence of man to endure the pressures of life.

John indicated this same truth when he wrote:

Now when {Christ} was in Jerusalem at the Passover, in the feast day, many believed in his name, when they saw the miracles which he did. But Jesus did not commit himself unto them, because he knew all men, And needed not that any should testify of man: for he knew what was in man (John 2:23–24).

Jesus could not commit Himself to those who were actually believing on Him, for He knew their belief was based upon their own observation. Their belief came out of their own "root system," and it would wilt under the hot sun of tribulation or persecution. Man simply does not have within himself the capability to exist continually. He "dureth [only] for a while." If the germinated seed is not allowed to take root, life will always wither away.

Who can hear? Notice what causes the problem for the man who hears with joy but "dureth for a while": ". . . for when tribulation or persecution ariseth because of the word, by and by he is offended." The offense came through the very Word that he received with joy. The pressure that made him want to flee arose when the Word eventually revealed to the hearer that life was only in the Word. The hearer first heard because he assumed it was good for the enhancement of his own life. He became offended when he heard the Word was not for his own personal use. He did not understand that the enhancement of life is always the enhancement of the Word.

This offense of the Word is illustrated by another event in the life of Jesus:

> *Many therefore of his disciples, when they had heard this, said, This is an hard saying; who can hear it? When Jesus knew in himself that his disciples murmured at it, he said unto them, Doth this offend you? . . . From that time many of his disciples went back, and walked no more with him* (John 6:60–61, 66).

What did Jesus say that was so offensive? Why did His disciples, who previously heard Him, now say, "Who can hear . . .?" What caused them to walk no more with Him? They heard, but they [endured] for only a while.

John explained the problem with the narrative of the event. Jesus said:

> *I am {the} bread of life. . . . As the living Father hath sent me, and I live by the Father: so he that eateth me, even he shall live by me. This is that bread which came down from heaven: not as your fathers did eat manna, and are dead: he that eateth of this bread shall live for ever* (John 6:48, 57–58).

The real question was, "Would His disciples live by eating Him (the bread of life), or would they attempt to live by eating the 'bread' (manna) that He would provide for them?" If they ate one, they would die. If they ate the other, they would live.

These revealing statements are the closing remarks of Jesus' long discourse in the synagogue at Capernaum. This particular discourse began when a group of people asked Jesus how He arrived there. He was last seen by these people on the other side of the sea, going up into a mountain. With no boat to cross the sea, they knew that some kind of miracle had probably occurred (John 6:15–25).

They were well aware of the miracle power of Jesus. They were following Him "because they saw his miracles which he did on them that were diseased" (John 6:2). They even participated in the miracle of the feeding of the five thousand (John 6:5–14). When they asked the question, "Rabbi, when camest thou hither?", they, no doubt, expected the story of another miracle.

What they received, however, was a startling statement: ". . . Verily, verily, I say unto you, Ye seek me, not because ye saw the miracles, but because ye did eat of the loaves, and were filled" (John 6:26). Did they want to see miracles? Yes. But more than seeing miracles, they wanted what the miracles would do for them.

Were they seeking Jesus, or were they seeking what Jesus could do for them? In the context of the entire discourse, did they want the "manna" in order that their bellies might be filled? Or did they want Jesus, the true bread of life?

They were ready to respond with joy when they thought the miracles of Jesus were to enhance their life. They "went back, and walked no more with him" (John 6:66) when they began to hear that life was only in His life, however. They were not interested in Jesus being their God, for their belly was their God. Although they heard at once with joy, sadly, their hearing soon became impaired. The Word became offensive, and they withered in the sun.

Turning from the Word

In the first response to the parable of the sower, the seed did not penetrate the soil because the mind had been blinded by the "god of this world" (2 Cor. 4:4). The hearers would not let the Word be set with their heart because of the much-traveled road of their mental assertiveness. When the activities of the mind become the basis of understanding, the "light of the glorious gospel of Christ [the Word]" cannot shine into the heart (2 Cor. 4:4).

In the second response, the seed penetrated the soil. The seed was not able to develop sufficient roots to produce an enduring plant, however. In the explanation, Jesus stated that the Word initially would be heard with joy, only to become offensive later. As long as the mind of man thought the Word would be beneficial to man's self-existence, the Word was heard. When the Word proclaimed that the Word alone was the source of life, however, the mind of man became offended and the withering process began.

In the third response, the encounter with the Word actually produced fruit. Yet something happened that made the once productive plant become unfruitful. The secret of the mysteries of grace revealed in this third response is the continual painful reality of every fall. It is the story of Lucifer, Adam and Eve, the nation of Israel, and the continuing struggle of the church today.

Notice the similarity of the phrases "he becometh unfruitful" (Matt. 13:22) and "that which they have shall be taken away" (Matt. 13:12). The truth hidden behind these statements is the reason Jesus taught in parables. It is the mystery of life itself.

When the disciples asked Jesus why was He speaking in parables, He answered:

> . . . *Because it is given unto you to know the mysteries of the kingdom of heaven, but to them it is not given. For whosoever hath, to him shall be given, and he shall have more abundance: but whosoever hath not, from him shall be taken away even that he hath. Therefore speak I to them in parables: because they seeing, see not; and hearing, they hear not, neither do they understand. And in them is fulfilled the prophecy of Esaias, which saith, By hearing ye shall hear, and not understand; and seeing ye shall see, and shall not perceive: For this people's heart is waxed gross, and their ears dull of hearing, and their eyes they have closed; lest at any time they should see with their eyes, and hear with their ears, and should understand with their heart, and should be converted, and I should heal them* (Matt. 13:11–15).

What makes this dreadful tale even more devastating is to realize whom Jesus was describing. He was referring to the children of Israel. Jesus was revealing the failure of the people of God.

VICTIMS OF THE BLESSINGS. Once blessed of God, they had become victims of their own blessings. In experiencing the undeserved blessings of God, they began to emphasize their own perceived importance. Paul described their erroneous belief in his letter to the Romans:

Behold, thou art called a Jew, and restest in the law, and makest thy boast of God, And knowest his will, and approvest the things that are more excellent, being instructed out of the law; And art confident that thou thyself art a guide of the blind, a light of them which are in darkness, An instructor of the foolish, a teacher of babes, which hast the form of knowledge and of the truth in the law (Rom. 2:17–20).

Their minds took the blessings of God, and they deceived themselves into thinking that they were "somebody." Thus their focus shifted away from God and onto themselves.

Paul spoke with "great heaviness and continual sorrow" in his heart " . . . for my brethren, my kinsmen according to the flesh" (Rom. 9:2,3), when he wrote about the tragedy of those who were at one time fruitful but now had become unfruitful. They once gladly received the Word, but then something occurred that choked the Word and prevented the production of fruit.

The Word is effective. Paul implied that although his kinsmen were now "accursed" (Rom. 9:3), they had been blessed for they were:

Israelites; to whom pertaineth the adoption, and the glory, and the covenants, and the giving of the law, and the service of God, and the promises; Whose are the fathers, and of whom as concerning the flesh Christ came . . . (Rom. 9:4–5).

He further stated that the reason his kinsmen who were once blessed but now accursed was "Not as though the word of God [had] taken none effect . . ." (Rom. 9:6). The Word is always effective in producing life in those who hear. Death always comes to those who do not hear. Just as in the parable of the sower, the Word had been spoken to the children of Israel, and it produced fruit in those who heard.

True vs. false. Paul stated it in this manner: "Not as though the word of God hath taken none effect. For they are not all Israel, which are of Israel" (Rom. 9:6). Being true Israel was not a product of a biological birth into the lineage of Israel but rather was based upon the promised Word of God. God had said to the tribe of Israel:

Wherefore say to the children of Israel, I am the Lord, and I will bring you out from under the burdens of the Egyptians, and I will rid you out of their bondage, and I will redeem you with a stretched out arm, and with great judgments: I will take you to me for a people, and I will be to you a God: and ye shall know that I am the Lord your God, which bringeth you out from under the burdens of the Egyptians (Exod. 6:6–7).

If all of Israel had only kept hearing the Word of God, all of them would have continued to be true Israel. Only a remnant remained as true Israel, however.

Even so then at this present time also there is a remnant according to the election of grace. And if by grace, then it is no more of works: otherwise grace is no more grace. But if it be of works, then is it no more grace: otherwise work is no more work. What then? Israel hath not obtained that which he seeketh for; but the election hath obtained it, and the rest were blinded (According as it is written, God hath given them the spirit of slumber, eyes that they should not see, and ears that they should not hear;) unto this day (Rom. 11:5–8).

Israel sought God as no other nation. Yet they did not find whom they were seeking. What caused them to fail? Jesus stated it was "because they seeing see not; and hearing they hear not, neither do they understand" (Matt 13:13). Paul stated ". . . God hath given them the spirit of slumber, eyes that they should not see, and ears that they should not hear. . . ." (Rom. 11:8). Most of Israel stumbled because they sought God in their own seeing and hearing. Paradoxically, to the degree they used their minds to understand, their minds became useless in understanding.

Paul continued to explain the paradox of Israel:

Neither, because they are the seed of Abraham, are they all children: but, in Isaac shall thy seed be called. That is, They which are the children of the flesh, these are not the children of God: but the children of the promise are counted for the seed. For this is the word of promise, At this time will I come, and Sara shall have a son (Rom. 9:7–9).

The difference between Isaac and Ishmael was not that Isaac was predestined before his birth to be the child of God. Nor was Ishmael predestined before his birth to be the child of bondage. *How* they were brought into the world is what determined that Isaac would be blessed and Ishmael would be cursed.

God was "allowed" to produce Isaac by His word: "For this is the word of promise, At this time will I come, and Sara shall have a son" (Rom. 9:9). On the other hand, the minds of Abraham and Sara decided to help God out in His promise and produced Ishmael—not by grace but by works. It was not the persons of Isaac or Ishmael in themselves that made them blessed or cursed. How they were produced is what made them what they were.

Paul further illustrated this principle:

And not only this; but when Rebecca also had conceived by one, even by our father Isaac; (For the children being not yet born, neither having done any good or evil, that the purpose of God according to election might stand, not of works, but of him that calleth;) It was said unto her, the elder shall serve the younger. As it is written, Jacob have I loved, but Esau have I hated (Rom. 9:10–13).

Isaac also had two sons. Two sons by one father, yet different results: "As it is written, Jacob have I loved and Esau have I hated." Jacob was not loved because he was Jacob, however. Neither was Esau hated because he was Esau:

For the children being not yet born, neither having done any good or evil, that the purpose of God according to election might stand, not of works, but of him that calleth (Rom. 9:11).

Before they were born, the purpose of God for their lives had already been set. Meaning Jacob would not be loved based upon his works. Nor would Esau be hated based upon his works.

Does this mean, then, that Jacob was blessed and Esau was doomed before they were born? No! It is not Jacob or Esau that are predetermined. God had elected before the foundation of the world that all men could have life by being set with the Son of God (Eph. 1; Col. 1:17).

The "election process" itself has been predetermined. According to the good pleasure of God's will, all men were predetermined to have their existence as "adopted" children of God (Eph. 1:1–23). All men were predetermined to experience life by being set with Him who is Life. The living Word, being set with man, produces the fruit of life in man.

As the parable of the sower stated, however, the Word often falls upon soil that is impenetrable, stony, or thorn infested. Jacob was not loved because he was Jacob or because he did good things. Neither was Esau hated because he was Esau or because he did bad things. The determining factor is the election process (life is only in the Way). If Jacob and Esau had allowed the Word to be set with their hearts, they both would have been blessed. The variable is always the condition of the soil.

One of the boxes (frames of reference) of man's mind that impedes the hearing of revelation in the Jacob-and-Esau story is the preconceived idea that love and hate are opposite terms. The opposite of love is not hate. Rather, it is apathy. If the opposite of love is found in a relationship, then there is actually no relationship. It is complete indifference to each other.

For hate to exist, there has to be a relationship. In a hate relationship, however, where love once existed, the relationship has become distorted. It has become depraved. One of the participants of a relationship has come to detest (the actual meaning of the word, which is translated *hate* in the New Testament) the other.

Usually it occurs when one assumes that the other has taken an unfair advantage over him. Esau assumed that Jacob had taken advantage of him. Sadly, the abhorrence he felt toward Jacob turned toward God, also.

Man constantly detests God's decree that life is only in the Son of God. He continually takes the blessings of life and then tries to live life by life itself. Or, as the parable of the sower indicated, life (the care of the world) is attempted to be experienced in the "deceitfulness of riches" (the blessings of life). Man is continually deceived into thinking that life itself is the producer of life. So, turning from the living Word, man constantly attempts to live by experiencing life in life itself.

Paul said, however, "So then it is not of him that willeth, nor of him that runneth, but of God that sheweth mercy" (Rom. 9:16). Life is not in the willing or the running, but it is in the receiving of the compassionate love of God. Experiencing life is not trying to live in the blessings, but rather it is consistently being set with the One who gives the blessings. Experiencing life is the experiencing of a person, Jesus Christ.

Choking the Word. When man attempts to live life in the blessings of life, he always becomes unfruitful. The thorns (cares of the world and the deceitfulness of riches) always "choke the word." Again, as Paul stated:

> *For the scripture saith unto Pharaoh, Even for this same purpose have I raised thee up, that I might shew my power in thee, and that my name might be declared throughout all the earth. Therefore hath he mercy on whom he will have mercy, and whom he will he hardeneth* (Rom. 9:17–18).

Pharaoh, himself, was not predetermined to be damned in order that God would show forth His power. Pharaoh, like everyone, had an opportunity to hear the Word.

When Moses came sharing the Word, however, Pharaoh's mind would not allow the Word to be set with his heart, and the hardening process began. Self-perception is the deadly disease that kills. As stated previously, a once-receptive heart that has been much traveled by the self-seeing of man's mind will become impenetrable. The power of God and His name is declared throughout all the earth not only by the life He produces but also by the death that occurs when the soil becomes impenetrable.

THE MAKING OF THE VESSEL. Paul's rousing question to the Romans illustrates the great truth of the parable of the sower. He stated, "Hath not the potter power over the clay, of the same lump to make one vessel unto honor, and another unto dishonor?" (Rom. 9:21). Notice it is not different lumps that make the difference. Out of the same lump vessels of honor and dishonor are made. Obviously, the difference is in how the vessels are made.

In other words, God has predestined the way vessels are made. If the way is not rejected, all men will be honorable. The rejection of the way, however, always produces dishonor. Moreover, this dishonor is not a production of man but the absence of God.

If the vessel is made by the Way (living by the Spirit), it will be a vessel unto honor. If the vessel becomes hardened and the Word does not penetrate the heart (living by the flesh), it becomes a vessel unto dishonor. Sadly, in the third response of the parable of the sower, a vessel that once was honorable had become dishonorable: ". . . the cares of the world and the deceitfulness of riches, choke the word, and he becometh unfruitful" (Matt. 13:22).

Alarmingly, in the parable of the sower, three of the four responses were negative. Jesus said, "For many are called, but few are chosen" (Matt. 22:14). Why is the overriding picture of the parable of the sower so negative? Why are so few chosen?

Man's mind will not let "the light of the glorious gospel of Christ, who is the image of God, shine [in his heart]" (2 Cor. 4:4). The self-assertiveness of the mind constantly resists the shining forth of the gospel into the heart. Man's mind will not let the Word be "set" with the heart.

Jesus said, "Who hath ears to hear, let him hear" (Matt. 13:9). The story line of the parable of the sower moved from not hearing at all, to hearing with a concealed motive, and finally to hearing that became deaf. Man consistently closes his spiritual eyes and his spiritual ears ". . . lest at any time they should see with their eyes, and hear with their ears, and should understand with their heart, and should be converted, and [be healed]" (Matt. 13:15).

Obstinate ego. It is not that man does not want to be converted from his never-ending failures or to be healed from his misery. Every man desires to live life to the fullest degree. Man wants to be his own savior and sustainer of life, however. Thus, he readily accepts a new program or suggestion regarding how he may enhance his life. He resists the message that he can do nothing for his salvation or to maintain his salvation, however. Jesus emphasized this truth when He said, "I am come in my Father's name, and ye receive me not: if another shall come in his own name, him ye will receive" (John 5:43).

All men (except Jesus) will run to hear an expert because the expert is perceived to have the answers of life. All men (except Jesus) will run to hear one who has made a name for himself, for he is currently perceived to be successful. All men (except Jesus) want to be the expert and to make names for themselves. Some just do it in the name of religion while others do it outside the church. Making a name for himself or for God comes out of the same tree of the knowledge of good and evil, however. It is the sad tale of self-assertiveness of the mind, the Lucifer Principle.

Journey of life. The self-actualization of man, either for himself or for God, always produces the negative results of the fleeting, withering, or dying life. It makes no difference where man may be on his journey of life. The moment the Word is prohibited from being set with the heart is the moment death begins.

The dying process is seen and experienced from the impenetrable ground, from the stony ground, and from the thorn-infested ground. It is seen from the much-traveled road of the self-seeing man, from the concealed motives of the selfish man, and from the deception of the self-made man. It is seen every time man begins to think and to believe in his own perceived intellect.

The hearing of the Word is the only prerequisite to a bountiful, fruitful life. John recorded, "No man hath seen God at any time; the only begotten Son, which is in the bosom of the Father, he hath declared him" (John 1:18). Out of the Father comes the divine expression, revealing the ways of God. To experience the Word is to experience life. Moreover, God the Father continually speaks to mankind through the living Word. It is a revelation that flows to all men.

Because of the "mind of man," some men will not let that glorious light shine into their hearts. The mind of man continually battles to impede the hearing process. Luke recorded, ". . . Jesus rejoiced in spirit, and said, I thank thee, O Father, Lord of heaven and earth, that thou hast hid these things from the wise and prudent, and hast revealed them unto babes . . ." (John 10:21). Truth is revealed to babes, but it is hidden from the wise and prudent.

Continuum of revelation. Every man (except Jesus Christ) consistently finds himself impeding the receiving of the revelation of God in his heart to some degree. The degree of impediment is in direct proportion to the activity of his mind. According to the parable of the sower, man has the capability of moving either backward or forward in his process of hearing the Word.

In the third response of the parable, man heard the Word, but later stopped hearing and became unfruitful (Matt. 13:22). He moved backward. In response to the disciples' question of why He spoke in parables, Jesus stated, "For whosoever hath, to him shall be given, and he shall have more abundance . . . [man moving forward]" (Matt. 13:12). He moves backward or forward on the continuum of revelation to the degree his mind hinders his heart opening up to the revelation process.

Man's backward or forward progress in hearing the Word is governed by the "self-activity" of his mind. If he has the mind of a child, he is more fully open to the revelation of God. He has a heart in which the glorious light of the gospel can penetrate, germinate, take root, and produce abundant fruit. The self-assertiveness (the much-traveled road) of the mind has not yet limited the opportunity to hear the Word. His mind is truly open. He has not yet tried to put God into a box.

If he has the mind of the "wise and learned" (a mind that has been developed to stand in its own intellectualism), he has a heart that is more difficult to be penetrated by the gospel because of the intellectualism of the mind. He has put God into a box so small that the gospel is prohibited from penetrating the heart. In fact, the size of the box seems to be the determining factor in the impediment of revelation to the heart. In the parable of the sower, the condition of the soil determined the response of the sowing of the seed.

Cultivation of the Heart

Obviously, the condition of the soil is extremely important. The mind of man will not let him understand how the soil is cultivated, however. Man consistently perceives that he has in his own capability the power to prepare the soil for the seed. Since the soil is the heart (spirit), and not the mind, there is nothing flesh can do to cultivate the heart. Since "that which is born of the flesh is flesh; and that which is born of the Spirit is spirit" (John 3:6), flesh and spirit will not mix. The flesh can do nothing to enhance the realm of the Spirit.

This is the reason Jesus stated, "Marvel not that I said unto thee, Ye must be born again" (John 3:7). Man attempting to live life in his own perceived capability (the flesh) must experience a complete turn-around. Jesus said, ". . . Verily, verily, I say unto thee, Except a man be born of water and of the Spirit, he cannot enter into the kingdom of God" (John 3:5).

He must be moved from being controlled by the flesh. He must come under the control of the Spirit. Man must experience repentance, a turnaround from the flesh to the Spirit. Obviously, if man needs to be saved from the flesh, then the flesh itself will have no positive participation in that salvation. The flesh never has a positive participation in entering into the kingdom of God or in continuing in the kingdom of God.

REPENTANCE. Perhaps the most urgent message to the church today is the call for repentance by the Holy Spirit. Unfortunately, the call for repentance is largely misunderstood by most. Correspondingly, if the knowledge of repentance is faulty, the act, or process, of repentance will also be faulty. Thus, true repentance rarely occurs, and the church continues to struggle in its life and its mission for Christ.

Why is repentance misunderstood by so many? One reason is that repentance is perceived as an act that an individual does. It is not perceived as a description of what God does as man experiences reconciliation. True repentance, however, is always a work of grace. Repentance is less an act that one does to enable God to restore him, than it is a description of the process that occurs when one is reconciled back to God.

To many, repentance erroneously means something they do in order to get God to forgive and restore them. They feel that if they confess their sins and turn away from them, God will forgive and reconcile. If indeed that explains repentance, the key principle behind repentance would be the individual's turning from sin. Moreover, the turning away from sin would then merit God's forgiveness. Thus, reconciliation could occur based upon a "work" that man did. Questions must be raised, however: Does man have the capability to turn from sin? Can man merit God's forgiveness?

Inadequate confession. Another difficulty in understanding repentance is the failure to understand what exactly should be repented of. In other words, when a Christian does something wrong, forgiveness should be sought. Rarely, however, is that repentance carried far enough. Forgiveness for the act of sin should be sought; however, the individual must also come under conviction and experience godly sorrow for the particular life-style that permitted the sin to occur.

Certainly forgiveness must be sought for an act of sin; however, of greater importance is the individual's seeking for forgiveness of his life-style. In fact, most of the time when sin occurs, it is a telltale sign that the individual, even though he may be a Christian, is going in the wrong direction in some aspect of his life. He probably has been trying to live for Christ, instead of allowing Christ to live in him.

A fresh look. The English words *repent*, *repentance*, and *repented* occur in the New Testament over sixty times. All three of these words come from the same compound Greek word. The prefix of this Greek term translated *repent*, *repentance*, and *repented* means "change," or "alteration." The root word itself means "to exercise the mind." Thus, the words *repent*, *repentance*, and *repented*, built upon the Greek term, would mean "to think differently," or "a change of mind on reflection." Consequently, implied in the very definition of repentance is the idea of turning from going in the wrong direction. It is a call to turn around, to think differently.

Why is repentance so difficult to experience? The basic reason is the call to repentance is a call to turn around. In other words, if repentance is needed, the church (or the individual) has developed a faulty course of action. The church (or the individual) must come back to the fork in the road where the wrong direction began. This call "to think differently" is difficult because it is a call to turn away from the current course of action of which the participants are so proud.

Repentance occurs only when the confession of error comes forth from the heart of man. Man had rather pray for God to help him from this point on, than to confess he has been wrong in the past. The confession that the wrong road has been traveled is extremely difficult for man's ego. It is difficult for the individual in his personal life. It is even more difficult for individuals in positions of leadership because it calls into question their leadership.

Godly repentance. Repentance is a turning from one direction toward the opposite direction. Repentance is more than a person saying he is sorry and attempting to turn away from his sins, however. God does not save man because he attempts to turn himself. Moreover, man does not have the capability to turn himself around.

Does the new Christian become a new creature in Christ because he turns himself away from sin? No! He becomes a new creature because Christ turns him around (John 1:12–13). Christ turns him around because he confesses he is a sinner headed in the wrong direction and cries out for help. He is turned around because he cries out to be saved from himself. Only when man comes to the end of himself will he cry out for salvation.

It is in one's helplessness, not in one's effort, that God saves man. Repentance, therefore, is more a description of what God does as man experiences reconciliation, than it is an act man does. Repentance is a work of God's grace.

When Peter proclaimed to the large crowd gathered at Pentecost, ". . . Repent, and be baptized every one of you in the name of Jesus Christ for the remission of sins. . . ." (Acts 2:38), he was simply saying, "Hey, you're going in the wrong direction. You need to come under the authority of Jesus, to be immersed in Him. You need to be turned around. Let Jesus bring you out from under your own control (repent) and be immersed (baptized) in the control of Jesus."

EXCHANGED LIFE. The people who heard Peter's message did not have the capability to turn their lives around, but Jesus did. When they confessed their sins and, more importantly, confessed the self-rule that produced those sins, Jesus came into their lives and gave them a new direction (John 1:11–13). They were changed from self-rule to Christ-rule.

Were the people of Israel who heard Peter's cry ready to hear the message? Luke recorded, "Then they that gladly received his word were baptized: and the same day there were added unto them about three thousand souls" (Acts 2:41). Repentance occurred because they "gladly received his word." No doubt the years of self-rule by the Pharisees had produced such misery in the life of the people that they were ready for the turnaround. Although the leadership of Israel resisted the message (Acts 4:1), the circumstances in the life of the people made them ready to hear.

Cultivating the soil. Amazingly, the preparation of the soil to hear the Word is always through the negative experiences of life itself. The failure to experience the life of the Word produces the death of man. The flesh manifested in the fleeting life of the impenetrable ground, the withering life of the stony ground, or the dying life of the thorn-infested ground does its deadly work. This pain of dying eventually cultivates man's soil to make him able to hear the Word.

The negative circumstances of life eventually drive man to cry out to God for his salvation. Ultimately, man desires a turnaround only when he comes to the end of himself, when his soil has been cultivated. God has so arranged that the circumstances of life become the basis for the eventual cultivation of the soil.

Complete deliverance. The cry for salvation must be a cry for complete deliverance, however. For, historically, man's cry for deliverance has consistently failed to be a cry for complete salvation. What started out to be such a powerful move of God toward total repentance becomes thwarted by man's self-preservation.

As man begins to experience the new, revitalizing wine of the Holy Spirit, it seems strange things begin to happen. Yes, new life begins to be experienced. Moreover, the old forms of death begin to be destroyed. As the old forms begin to be destroyed, however, fear strikes the mind. The very things the mind had used for its expression of life are now being taken away.

The mind begins to understand the consequences of the coming of new wine. It begins to perceive that in order for the old forms to be destroyed, the mind must die to its own expressions (the old forms). The mind cannot tolerate its own death, however. The cry for deliverance mellows, and the emphasis shifts from the continual flow of new wine to the "patching of the old forms."

God's life. Every man (except Jesus) will always resist to the last ounce of life within his being, the completed work of Christ—the outpouring of new wine and the destruction of the old forms. Every man (except Jesus) wants life, but he wants to experience it within his own being, within the expressions of his mind. Life—abundant life—comes forth only in the soil where the pure Word is continually being set. For God does not give man life to experience as his own. God only allows man to experience His life. "Who hath ears to hear, let him hear" (Matt. 13:9).

> *. . . Behold, a sower went forth to sow; And when he sowed, some seeds fell by the way side, and the fowls came and devoured them up: Some fell upon stony places, where they had not much earth: and forthwith they sprung up, because they had no deepness of earth: And when the sun was up, they were scorched; and because they had no root, they withered away. And some fell among thorns; and the thorns sprung up, and choked them: But other fell into good ground, and brought forth fruit, some an hundredfold, some sixtyfold, some thirtyfold. Who hath ears to hear, let him hear. And the disciples came, and said unto*

him, Why speakest thou unto them in parables? He answered and said unto them, Because it is given unto you to know the mysteries of the kingdom of heaven, but to them it is not given. For whosoever hath, to him shall be given, and he shall have more abundance: but whosoever hath not, from him shall be taken away even that he hath. Therefore speak I to them in parables: because they seeing see not; and hearing they hear not, neither do they understand. And in them is fulfilled the prophecy of Esaias, which saith, By hearing ye shall hear, and shall not understand; and seeing ye shall see, and shall not perceive: For this people's heart is waxed gross, and their ears are dull of hearing, and their eyes they have closed; lest at any time they should see with their eyes, and hear with their ears, and should understand with their heart, and should be converted, and I should heal them. But blessed are your eyes, for they see: and your ears, for they hear. For verily I say unto you, That many prophets and righteous men have desired to see those things which ye see, and have not seen them; and to hear those things which ye hear, and have not heard them. Hear ye therefore the parable of the sower (Matt. 13:3–18).

The secret of the rich, full, contented life is always in the simple living of life. Since there is mystery in the living of life, however, man rarely, if ever, experiences the life he so desperately desires. A quick, honest look at one's existence readily reveals a life that falls short of the expectations of the continual good life. Regardless of his efforts, man always seems to fall short of perfection, the complete life.

Failing to grasp the truth of living in God's grace, man spends his days in an abnormal existence. Moreover, this abnormality (experiencing life less than God intended it to be) is so consistent that man has come to accept it as the norm. This deception has become so entrenched within man's mind that it prohibits him from rising above the all-too-frequent hells of his life.

Moreover, in order to prevent total insanity within himself, the deception of his mind has created a sense of self-worth, by measuring and comparing the doing of himself to the doing of others. Sadly, success in this abnormal life is always measured at the expense of others. Unfortunately, man has a sense of worth within himself, only if he perceives that he is doing better than someone lower than himself.

Life, continually experiencing complete (fulfilled) existence in peace and joy (Rom. 14:17), can only come to man from outside of the working of his mind. Man cannot come to know truth from within his own framework of existence. Although truth always comes to man in the experiences of life, it is never the experiences of life that brings him truth. Truth is only ascertained by man as he encounters Jesus in his life. The true way of life can only come by the pure revelation of Jesus Christ, the revelation of grace.

Unfortunately, most people of the world, including most Christians, struggle in life because they never get past this simple, yet profound, challenge of grace and its revelation. They never seem to experience even the beginning of grace in their lives. They consistently experience the frustration of grace by their own attempt to do rather than to be. They do not see or understand the revelation of grace.

The story continues.

VOLUME TWO: *Conquered by Jesus*

Salvation is the story of what God does for man in spite of man. Man's intellect, once his glory but now his shame, has such control over him that he literally has to be conquered by Jesus. It is only in the innocence of man's mind that the grace of God continually flows, enabling him to experience the life of God. Moreover, man not only has to be dragged back to God; he also has to be driven to others to enable him to experience the manifestation of Jesus between them. Jesus is the only way that the exercise of the mind, that which produces the devil (see Matt. 16:23—*savorest* means to exercise the mind), can be conquered.

When man does not experience the life of God as it was meant to be, he continually turns to his own activities to attempt to produce life. Paul identified three of these activities as "worship, humility, and self-denial" (Col. 2:23). To the degree that one believes that these activities will produce life, that's the degree of anticipation and excitement that the activities produce when they are practiced. However, to the same degree, frustration will occur when these activities eventually fail. Although God has warned man not to bow down or serve "any graven images" (Exod. 20:4–5), man continually creates new idols that will supposedly produce the good life.

Just as the darkness is real only in the fact that light is absent, these idols only seem real because the life of Jesus is absent. These images created by man's mind actually have power, only because man gives the idols his allegiance. In other words, man's own mind gives the powerless idol power over him. Man can have a deep emotional experience from the worship of an idol because his own mind produces the emotions.

This pursuit of life by man produces the need for salvation. It is not the activities themselves from which man must be saved. Man must be saved from himself. He must be saved from placing himself at the center of his universe, even though all of his pursuits may be directed toward God.

Only in the innocence *(innocence* means freedom from guilt or sin through being unacquainted with evil: blameless—*Webster's Collegiate Dictionary,* 10th Edition) of man's mind does the grace of God (supernatural enablement to be) continually flow, enabling man to experience the life of God. This revelation of grace brings man to his salvation. Jesus came to take man to a place where He would go and prepare for him (John 14:2). It is a place of rest—horizontal and passive, as opposed to vertical and active, which causes man to fade out of sight until only Christ is seen (John 15:16). The Father has sent His Son into the world of the believer to baptize him with His Spirit to take him where he could not go himself. It is the mission of grace to save man from himself. Man must be conquered by Jesus.

VOLUME THREE: *Connections of Life*

Two opposing principles are at work in the lives of all people. Although most people enhance themselves at the expense of others (the Lucifer Principle), the rich, full, and complete life can be experienced only when an individual enhances others at his expense (the Jesus Principle). Abundant life is only experienced in others.

Even when others become the object of kind, loving, and benevolent actions, the mystery of life is still not understood. Others are not to be the object of one's life. In the mystery of what it means to be created in the image of God, others are actually the person's ground of being. What it means to be a person cannot be defined in the light of an isolated individual.

God is One, but He is Three-in-One. Connection in love, the manifestation of Jesus in the relationship of two people (oneness in three-ness) is the connection of life. It is the only way to experience the rich, full, and complete life.

If the most alarming error in modern Christianity is the failure to perceive Jesus as the breath and heartbeat of life itself, the second staggering failure is the perception of where Jesus is actually manifested. Much of Christianity today (especially in the culture of the West) simply does not realize the only manifestation of Jesus that can occur in one's life will always be in the connections of relationships. Jesus is experienced in the mystery of oneness in three-ness. He is experienced in the connections of life.

This life of Jesus in the connections of life can be illustrated by the parable of the mustard seed:

> *It is like a grain of mustard seed, which, when it is sown in the earth, is less than all the seeds that be in the earth: But when it is sown, it groweth up, and becometh greater than all herbs, and shooteth out great branches; so that the fowls of the air may lodge under the shadows of it* (Mark 4:31–32).

Connections of life, when they begin are like the smallest of seeds planted in one's life. Yet, if the relationship is allowed to grow to maturity, the process, the growing together of two to become one, becomes the greatest event of their lives.

The germinating relationship between a man and a woman, the most basic connection of life, becomes the ground of being for each other. When both members of the relationship are continually experiencing the growing process of the relationship, the knowing of each other then becomes a never-ending noble adventure in the experiencing of life. The joy of life is always in the knowing of another.

Moreover, the relationship that is formed between the man and the woman actually becomes greater than the sum of the two individuals. It radiates life not just to the two but to all those who "may lodge under the shadows of it." It is the true witness of believers. It is the manifestation of Jesus in the connections of life.

VOLUME FOUR: **Mysteries of Baptism**

There has been only one man who has died and has been resurrected to never die again: Jesus Christ. Failing to recognize the significance of that truth, many people ignorantly try to live for themselves, or even try to live for God. Although the resurrected life of Jesus may be seen in the lives of all men, they cannot produce it by their physical effort or mental exercise.

Even trying to believe that one is dead through Jesus is futile. For only being "baptized for the dead" by Jesus enables man to experience the life of Jesus. In other words, God continually brings man to his "dying off" (the actual meaning of the English *dieth*, *death*, and *dead* when they are associated with man in the New Testament) that he may experience the "raising up" of Jesus in his life.

When man attempts to raise himself by his own deeds (physical or mental); he always frustrates the grace of God. Tragically, it has always been the people of God who eventually fail to experience continually the rich, full, and complete life of God. In other words, the relationship between most believers and Christ, incredibly, soon stagnates and ceases to be the exciting adventure that it had been.

The relationship becomes stale and lifeless, a deadly boredom. Since the individual is no longer experiencing the full, rich, and complete life of God, he becomes subject to temptation, to find life somewhere else. He will even become more devoted to the increased effort of his activities to find life.

The secret of life is contained in the mysteries of baptism, however. Jesus said:

> *Verily, verily, I say unto you, Except a corn of wheat fall into the ground and die, it abideth alone: but if it die, it bringeth forth much fruit. He that loveth his life shall lose it: and he that hateth his life in this world shall keep it unto life eternal* (John 12:24–25).

Unless man continually experiences the dying off of self (the dying off of his activities), he cannot experience the vitality of the quickening power of God.

The mysteries of "being baptized into Jesus Christ [being] baptized into his death . . ." (Rom. 6:3) to experience ". . . the likeness of his resurrection" (Rom. 6:5) is the essence of life. The believer can never experience the death of actually being dead until he experiences the grave. He can experience the continual "dying off" of his life to experience the "raising up" of Jesus in this life before he goes to the grave, however.

The continual life of Jesus is made manifest in the believer's mortal body, but only if his life is never attempted in his mortal body, in his self-centeredness. The believer is alive but dying, yet dying he lives. It is a work of God, the mysteries of baptism. *Mysteries of Baptism* portrays the continual struggle of man to believe that Jesus is the sole essence of his life.

VOLUME FIVE: *Being Set Free*

The actual mechanics of man's creation would cause man to become a creature of two worlds. Being formed out of the dust of the ground, he is of this earthly realm, a temporal, flesh and blood person. Moreover, when God breathed into his nostrils the breath of life, he began to experience the heavenly realm. With the breath of life being the Spirit of God, man now experienced the eternal, spiritual essence of life. Through the mysteries of the incarnation, man became a vessel animated by the Spirit of God.

Although man has a corruptible, dishonorable, weak, natural body, he can experience the incorruptible, glorious, powerful, spiritual reality of the life of God. His mortality can be "swallowed up" by God's immortality. Being set free from the control and influences of the earthly realm, he can experience the life of the heavenly realm. He can be a spiritual being.

Jesus, "the way, the truth, and the life" (John 14:6), can set the spirit of man free from his earthly tabernacle. With each believer "receiv[ing] the Spirit of adoption, whereby [he can cry] Abba, Father" (Rom. 8:15), he can expect fully "the redemption of [his] body." With redemption meaning "ransom in full, i.e. riddance," "the redemption of {his} body" (Rom. 8:23), the believer can be loosed from the "earthly house of [his] tabernacle" (2 Cor. 5:1). The believer can be rid of any control whatsoever of the flesh. His spirit can be set free to experience "the glorious liberty of the children of God" (Rom. 8:21).

Man can continually experience the realm of the Spirit unless he falls to the fatal deception that he can direct his life by the choices of his own mind. Being deceived that he is free to make choices for good or evil, man is then forced to live by those choices. The exercise of man's mind has always produced his hells, has always produced an existence of the earthly realm.

Man was created with a freedom, but it was not the perceived freedom of choice that came with eating the fruit of the tree of the knowledge of good and evil. If man was created free to choose, and he chose to follow God, he would have a right to boast of his choice. He was not created free to choose good or evil (the perception after eating of the fruit of the tree of the knowledge of good and evil) but rather free to fall from God's grace. Man's freedom lies in the fact that he could move away from the tree of life, even to find himself at the foot of the tree of the knowledge of good and evil ready to eat.

In other words, man could do nothing to get life. It was given to him. He could frustrate that life, however. Not by a choice, for who chooses not to live but by deception? The issues of life are never matters of choice or chance, but matters of truth and deception. Man lives in the freedom of the spirit and experiences the continual flow of grace only in the innocence of his mind. *Being Set Free* portrays the struggle of man to live continually in the tree of life.

VOLUME SIX: *Reaching the Heart*

Like the threading of the smallest of needles, the essence of life is difficult to perceive with the natural eye. Moreover, the early believers in Christ seem to imply that understanding life is impossible by the mind of man. With such statements as ". . . ye need not that any man teach you . . ." (1 John 2:27) and ". . . I neither received it of man, neither was I taught it" (Gal. 1:12), the early believers indicated the secrets of life have nothing to do with the intellect of man.

Marvelously, the receiving of truth, understanding the mysteries of life, is a spiritual encounter with Truth. The life of God is only experienced when the believer stands faith to faith, glory to glory, face to face, or heart to heart with God. It is never a process of the human mind. It is having a heart for God.

The continual, direct experiencing of Jesus Christ is the only prerequisite for life. Jesus said:

> *Verily, verily, I say unto you, He that heareth my word, and believeth on him that sent me, hath everlasting life, and shall not come into condemnation; but is passed from death unto life. Verily, verily, I say unto you, the hour is coming, and now is, when the dead shall hear the voice of the Son of God: and they that hear shall live* (John 5:24–25).

The experiencing of life is the experiencing of Jesus, hearing Him directly.

Ultimately, the experiencing of life is the experiencing of Jesus in the heart. Truth sets man free. Truth is not a body of knowledge to be ascertained by the mind, however. Truth is a Person to be encountered with the heart.

When man attempts to know the truth of God by the mind, he always puts another man between himself and God. Whether it is his own intellect (his self-centeredness), or even a Moses (as did the children of Israel), putting a man in a vertical hierarchy between the soul and God is disastrous. The Promised Land, the life of God, is never obtained.

Man cannot produce life in another man, even if he is speaking the Word of God. For example, the children of Israel desired not to hear God directly, heart to heart, but rather to hear Moses as he shared what God had told him. Tragically, neither Moses nor the people made it into the Promised Land. Ultimately, life cannot be experienced, even by the sharing of truth as a body of knowledge. Truth is not information. Truth is a Person, Jesus Christ.

Experiencing life is experiencing Jesus directly. Life has no grandchildren. The journey of life for every individual is always his own personal journey to Jesus.

Reaching the Heart explores the mysteries of encountering Truth. It examines why man continually turns to his mind for guidance and the hell it always produces. It shares the gospel that ultimately reveals how God intended for man to live.

To order additional copies of

Journey to Jesus
Volume One: Quest for Life

Have your credit card ready and call

(877) 421-READ (7323)

or send $10.95 each plus $3.95* S&H to

**WinePress Publishing
PO Box 428
Enumclaw, WA 98022**

* add $1.00 S&H for each additional book ordered